REVIEW

A much needed, evidence based state of the union on personality testing in the workplace. Essential reading to balance the hype and disinformation flooding the market, it explains where we are with personality tests, how we got here, and what needs to happen next to put it right. **Nik Kinley, Director, YSC Consulting**

This book works at pace through theory, insight, and thought-provoking hooks within the world of personality testing. Having been the champion and often a victim of many a personality test, this book supports my current view: mistrust the marketing hype of big prediction. Andrew Munro combines theory and practical insight beautifully, not over playing one or the other. I would recommend this book to those at each stage of their professional HR or Talent Management journey: Just starting out and conforming to the norms and practices to earn your stripes. Be cautious. Don't jump in. Use your judgement. In mid-career and relying on the "usual" without thinking why you began using personality testing in the first place. Think about all those people you have recruited. Have you ever reviewed the information once they enter the organisation? I bet 90% of the profiles were never seen again. Those like me who have more years behind them in their career than ahead. Even the old ones learn new insights. **Jackie Kelly, Group HR Director, Watkin Jones Group**

A compelling, evidence based analysis of personality tests and whether they actually measure or deliver on what they claim to. It effectively challenges the uncanny intuitive appeal of personality tests and their purported usefulness in the workplace. **Shahana Banerjee, CEO, Just Human | Not Resources**

For decades, Andrew Munro has been a voice of reason in an overly commercialised and sometimes fraudulent industry. Munro has condensed years of common sense in this short read that takes the reader through the essence of the problem - we aren't predicting much at all. For those unfamiliar with the field they could do a lot worse than absorb the lessons in the section Future Directions.

"Among the competing products developed by psychologists, perhaps the most important are their assessment instruments. Unfortunately, in psychology we have no consumers union to test competing claims and to compare these products on their overall effectiveness. The testing industry provides minor cosmetic successive variants of the same product where only the numbers after the names substantially change. These variants survive because psychologists buy the tests and then loyally defend them." Compulsory reading for HR professionals. Be informed and be part of the solution, not the problem. **Paul Englert, Executive Coach and Psychologist, Organisational and Individual Transformation, Pracademic**

An accessible, pacey introduction for non-specialists to the perils of psychometric personality profiling. **Dr Steve Blinkhorn, Managing Director, Psychometric Research & Development Ltd**

This book deserves to be widely read by HR professionals, search and selection advisors and, of course those who specialise in psychometrics within the testing industry. In addition to looking back at the history and high expectations of the past, the malaise of the middle years, it addresses ambitions in a world of AI. It is a comprehensive and compulsive read.

The book also calls to explore techniques worth revisiting through fresh eyes. Simply jettisoning all existing instruments will however not happen - if ever and certainly not quickly. Building on this evidence, what is required for a more sophisticated approach to the core issue of selection?

Outsourcing the hard thinking to any one or more instruments is a lazy response. This book restarts a wider and better informed debate about our current selection practices. What are we selecting for, and how do we gain evidence of the likely success of the selected? How do we ensure successful transitions in those post-selection pre arrival and early days in a new role? Personality assessment alone was never was the answer to the exam question. This book joins the dots on the severe limitations of a practice which we once believed to be an answer. **Dr Tom Kennie, Director, Ranmore Consulting**

As a profession, HR seems particularly prone to falling in love with the next new idea. Too often we have fast solution fever. The increasing volume and pace of work makes marketing hype all the more tempting. I find it increasingly challenging to get leaders to focus on the root causes of the problems they are trying to solve and get clear on the outcomes they want to lead for. Activity trumps thoughtfulness. Assessment and selection practices seem particularly prone to this. The consolidation of the providers within the sector and the commodification of integrated assessment solutions also hasn't encouraged us to get under the hood of the engines we're deploying. This is particularly problematic as organisational culture and diversity become such key dynamics in the increasing scramble for talent. How personality tools contribute or at worst create bias is difficult to discern. Why do we accept this?

This book does a fantastic job of reminding and inspiring us not to be so complacent in following familiar ways of thinking - but to be more questioning of the candidate experience we want to create and the predictive outcomes we are trying to achieve. The background to the development of the field and depth of research charting the reality of the outcomes is truly sobering. Definitely one to share with my team.
Jayne Antrobus, Group Head of Talent, Marks and Spencer

Personality testing is a proverbially fraught topic. It is a confusing morass of claims and counterclaims, often based on scant evidence and difficult-to-understand statistical models. But who can say no to the promise of an easy-to-administer, low-cost, and accurate guide to employee success? Judged by the number of tests and the annual market for personality tests, very few of us.

This book is a transparent, logical, unbiased, and easy-to-read treatise shining a bright and insightful light on the complex, often contradictory world of personality testing. Who should read this book? Psychology students interested in researching personality. Test publishers wanting to improve their tools. Organisational psychologists who use or are considering adding personality measures to their selection processes. Consultants advising the former. Anyone interested in understanding what all the fuss is about.

Munro writes in plain, clear English, makes the logic of his arguments clear, and is fair to the pros and cons of personality measures. In keeping with his penchant for pithy quotes, I'll offer a bastardisation of Samuel Johnson: *Personality testing is like a dog walking on his hind legs. It is not done well; but you are surprised to find it done at all*. **Bruce Sevy, PhD, Founder, Talent Strategy Consulting**

A sophisticated challenge to the uncritical dissemination and use of the personality questionnaire. It displays a masterly grasp of the academic literature, examining the validity when it comes to predicting performance whilst acknowledging a carefully selected regime of ability tests has demonstrable predictive validity for job performance. Written with pungent wit about the credibility of personality questionnaires to do the same, and sceptical about those in the trade who peddle tools that do not predict performance but claim they do. A big challenge to HR Departments to get it right rather than throw the baby out with bath water. **Dr Rob Irving, Founding Partner, The Talent Alliance**

This is a truly comprehensive and thought-provoking analysis of this complex topic. Its very well informed and rigorous approach to the subject by a leading expert will give all who use this type of test a great deal to consider and to act upon when they read it. **David Bannister, Director Scotwork International**

I loved reading this, and am geeky enough to say I "couldn't put it down". One might be tempted to look at Andrew Munro's role as contrarian to stimulate critical assessment of our field in the process. He is good at that. In this case, I see him as being very mainstream, representing what the vast majority of our colleagues would support in the domain of personality assessment. And he is good at this too. We all need to be critical of the claims of our ability to predict performance, with a strong eye towards those who have some vested interest in the benefits of those claims. This book provides a well-organised map for navigating this terrain. This situation is only going to get worse as AI creates an even darker shroud over the inner workings of supposed algorithms.

Much of my motivation to read and consume this content is that I am now teaching assessments to graduate students, and would love to make this part of their reading list. **Dave Bracken Ph.D. DWBracken & Associates**

Andrew Munro's book, Personality Testing in Employee Selection is a thought provoking journey into the intricate world of personality testing. Having been immersed in this field for quite a long time, I approached the book with some preconceived notions. However, I learned a great deal about this topic that I wasn't previously aware of - made clear through an informative and engaging style.

The book transcends the typical exploration of what personality testing entails and delves into the challenges and controversies that have surrounded it for decades. The author's meticulous examination of research evidence and critical assessment of the various aspects of personality testing leaves no stone unturned.

What sets this book apart is its ability to encourage readers, even those experienced in the field, to rethink their perspectives. It doesn't just dissect the issues; it provides a road map for potential solutions and future directions. I'd highly recommend this book to anybody who has interest in personality testing generally. Andrew is a true expert in this area, and I'm certain you'll learn a great deal. **Richard Anderson, Co-Founder Evolve Assess**

This critique of the use of psychometric testing for employee selection exposes the practice as something of a pseudoscience, almost the contemporary equivalent of the use of phrenology - the measurement of bumps on a person's skull - of the late 18th and early 19th centuries. The author identifies five flaws in the thinking behind the use of such tests; lack of validation, respondent self-deception, faking, inadequate theory, and problematic integration with selection decision-making.

Munro's conclusion that a fundamental rethink is required is entirely appropriate. How a person thinks and how they behave are still pivotal to how they perform at work. **Nick Shannon, Director at Management Psychology Ltd**

ABOUT THE AUTHOR

Andrew Munro (MA, C Psychol, AFBPS) is the lead Director at Talent World Consulting, a network of experienced practitioners providing services in design, implementation and evaluation across a range of applications in assessment, learning and development, performance management, coaching, talent reviews and succession planning.

He began his career in the world of psychometric testing. Andrew has also worked in financial services, responsible for corporate management education and development, and the integration of performance management, career management and succession planning for senior executives.

He draws on over 30 years' consulting experience across the corporate, public and third sectors. Assignments have run the spectrum from designing recruitment processes for front-line employees in retail, an evaluation of the knowledge test for London cab drivers, the validation of selection systems, organisational restructures and redeployment, implementing career and talent development programmes, through to Board level succession. Andrew has also collaborated on over 150 off-the-shelf and bespoke product applications for individual, team and organisational diagnostics and tool-kits.

He has published in the field of business psychology (Personnel Review; Selection & Development Review; Executive Development, Assessment and Development Matters).

Andrew is the author of Practical Succession Management, Now It's About Time, and co-author of A to Z and Back Again: Part 1 Adventures and Misadventures in Talent World, and Leadership Skills for Dental Professionals: Begin Well to Finish Well.

He can be contacted: andrew@amazureconsulting.com and www.talentworldconsulting.com.

PERSONALITY TESTING IN EMPLOYEE SELECTION

Challenges, Controversies and Future Directions

Andrew Munro

CONTENTS

OVERVIEW

Is it possible, he thinks, that nothing true and important has been seen, recognised or said? Is it possible that in spite of inventions and progress, in spite of culture, religion and worldly wisdom, one has remained on the surface? Yes, it is possible. **Rainer Maria Rilke**

Personality testing is a big business. It has an estimated global market value of £4 billion. There are now hundreds of vendors distributing and selling an array of tests - 1,319 at the last count - deployed across a range of applications. Personal and team development, vocational guidance, career counselling, executive coaching and employee selection draw on personality tests. The outcomes of this testing enterprise shape lives in important ways.

My daughter is really upset and angry. The manager has been profiling staff at staff meetings using a colour based personality tool. She objected to it but it has to comply. Her profile is totally incorrect.[1]

Personality testing has become increasingly common in the recruitment process. A report from CEB indicates that 62% of Human Resources departments now use personality tests to vet candidates during the hiring process.

The central issue that led to the disfavour of personality tests 40 years ago, the lack of predictive validity or the extent to which the assessment predicts job performance, still remains an unresolved issue. **Peter Capelli, Professor of Management at The Wharton School**

This book was prompted by a client who asked: **does personality testing work in selection?**

This question generated a series of posts on social media, which in turn became an article downloaded by thousands, and followed by encouraging comments to express similar reservations. In a few instances, the article attracted the ire of test publishers and practitioners whose commercial interests hinge on the sale of personality assessments and who objected to the analysis.

This book updates and consolidates the original research and feedback. This is not an academic paper. It is a book for the thinking practitioner looking for an informed view of options in recruitment and selection but who remains baffled by ongoing challenges and controversies in personality assessment. The book incorporates extensive notes and references to key scholars and experts in the field who have argued for and against the usage of personality testing in employee selection.

A range of academic researchers and expert practitioners have reviewed earlier drafts of articles and posts on LinkedIn to point out any shortcomings as well as provide constructive feedback and suggestions for improvement. None of whom are responsible for this interpretation of the consolidated research and commentary.

What does it mean for personality testing to work anyway? A more helpful question would be: *which specific tests work in which selection scenarios?*[2] Given the vast number of available tests and the different ways in which test data can be deployed within a range of selection processes, this doesn't lend itself to a simple evaluation.

This book addresses the broad sweep of findings in this field to summarise the challenges and controversies[3] for personality testing in the high stakes scenario of employee selection. The application of personality tests in personal and team development is not covered. The book reviews the evidence base to examine claims for the predictive validity of personality tests and outlines future directions for improved practice. As with most things in life, to make sense of the future it helps to revisit the past. The origins and evolution of personality testing are therefore revisited.

The words I really like most people I meet flash on to my screen, as the computer asks me how strongly I might agree or disagree with that statement. Welcome to the world of the psychometric test, for which the top prize could be a bank chairmanship and bags of class A drugs.[4]

The proposal is that self report personality measures have had over a century to demonstrate practical value in employee selection. Initial promising signs have not been translated into selection gains with significant organisational impact. The predictive power of personality testing has not improved over decades of sustained effort. If anything, it has declined.[5]

There has been a proliferation of tests to offer greater choice for the practitioner, but without a corresponding raising of the game - one seen in other competitive domains. Something odd is going on. And when ChatGTP4 is creating havoc in the testing market for cognitive aptitude, are the days of personality profiling in selection now numbered?

Using AI, like ChatGPT, to complete aptitude tests is technically possible. **ChatGPT**

This article outlines five reasons for the state of play:

- fundamental problems within the **validation research**.
- the realities of **self deception** and why we shouldn't expect too much insight from self report measures.
- how **faking** in applicant scenarios affects selection decision making, and why solutions to minimise, detect or mitigate faking have largely failed.
- the **lack of theory** to connect personality to performance. The complexities of context, cause and consequence make a simple theory unlikely. But there has been a remarkable lack of theoretical advancement to guide professional practice.
- the hazards of integrating personality test data within **selection decision making** and why the growing shift towards algorithms may be the problem not the solution to more systematic applications.

There are three responses to the disappointing predictive power of personality tests:

- **abandonment** to accept that the personality testing enterprise should now be dismantled. The game is well and truly up.

- **incremental improvement** to search for marginal gains that will establish personality testing's value in future selection. The game goes on, but new tactics are required.
- a **fundamental rethink** to explore alternatives to the instruments provided by the conventional test publishers. A new game needs to be played.

While the personality measures used in organisations should do better now than years ago, there is not much evidence that they are better. **Kevin Murphy**

And until we shift to:

- **contextualised and customised measures**.
- the addition of **objective metrics** rather than rely only on subjective self report measures.
- the greater use of image-based assessments for a more **engaging candidate experience** that avoids repetitive tedium.
- personality assessments that are **genuinely inclusive**; tests that aren't designed and validated only with WEIRD samples - Western, Educated, Industrialised, Rich, and Democratic.

we can only anticipate another century of counter-productive debate and confusing claims in which self report personality test data from applicants continue to account for next to zero variance in work performance. Or, at worst, businesses continue to apply tests that undermine organisational productivity and innovation.

THE AMAZING JAMES RANDI PSYCHOMETRIC AWARD

Uri Geller may have psychic powers by means of which he can bend spoons. If so, he appears to be doing it the hard way. **James Randi**

In 1964 the precursor to the $1 Million Paranormal Challenge was announced by James Randi,[6] a sceptic of the paranormal. Randi had achieved publicity in the 1970s by questioning the spoon bending claims of Uri Geller. Randi's offer: $1 million to any practitioner of the paranormal who could show evidence of any paranormal, supernatural, or occult power or event under proper observing conditions. Over a thousand people applied to take it. None were successful. The challenge was terminated in 2015.

In a variation of the Randi prize, a post appeared on LinkedIn a few years ago. This James Randi Psychometric Award would be given to the test publisher who provided evidence of the genuine business impact of any personality test in a selection context. The conditions were demanding but straightforward:

- a **base rate** of current selection success is available. A benchmark is needed to allow comparisons of improvements in impact.
- the results of the personality test were **not made available at the time of selection** to influence selection decision making. This avoids any bias in subsequent evaluations of performance.
- a decent **sample size**, modestly set at more than 150.
- successful candidates were tracked, and meaningful **performance data** linked to tangible business outcomes - sales, productivity, service, etc - were obtained after a year. Objective criteria of work outcomes of organisational importance was a requirement.

The debate was largely informative and good humoured. Contributors posted up references to a variety of research studies. The posts also highlighted some of the methodological issues involved in this kind of evaluation. A handful of posts suggested that the criteria were unreasonable. One angry test publisher argued that this requirement in research design and evaluation was unethical. Here the argument ran: *Of course personality testing works, and it would be highly irresponsible not to use the tests to improve selection.*

No doubt this kind of research methodology is difficult.[7] But given the proliferation of personality tests over the last century, someone, somewhere must have conducted a randomised control trial in an applicant context. Mustn't they?

As the discussion progressed over several weeks it became clear that no publisher or practitioner was either able or willing to provide evidence indicative of **any** incremental gain on current selection processes in an applicant context. This is odd. The verdict on personality testing in the 1950s to 1970s might have been: *it is difficult to advocate with a clear conscience the use of personality measures in most situations as a basis for making employment decisions about people.*[8] But after past challenges and controversies, the narrative had become that several meta-analytic studies throughout the 1990s had established the validity of personality instruments. So confident were the personality testers that one of the pioneers of the new wave of personality research announced that researchers and practitioners can now put *troubling matters and concerns aside.*

For the personality testers, the question is not: do *personality tests work?* Here the response has been an emphatic yes they do. The more pressing questions are now: which specific tests work best, where and when, and how best to optimise their value in selection? So why does the Psychometric James Randi

Award still remain open? To understand why, we go back in time and look at the beginnings of personality testing in employment selection.

ONCE UPON A TIME IN THE PAST

Military Beginnings

Personality testing, at least in a form recognisable today - self report through a questionnaire format - can be tracked back to 1917 and the design of an instrument to identify those soldiers likely to have nervous breakdowns. Originally an interview guide to screen out those candidates who might be emotionally unstable and unfit for active combat, this check-list evolved into a self report questionnaire: the Woodworth Personal Data Sheet.

A pragmatic decision was made. A questionnaire format would be much less expensive and time-consuming than an interview from a military psychiatrist. In a yes-no format, the test included questions of the type:

Does it make you uneasy to sit in a small room with the door shut?
Do you feel like jumping off when you are on a high place?
And the extraordinary: *Did you ever have St Vitus's Dance?* with the bizarre note, *Sydenham's Chorea - you would know.*

After the 1st World War, the author of the test identified opportunities to apply the test for the business sector. This test - the grandfather of all present day personality tests - met an emerging organisational need to *root out the undesirable and unstable workers.* The marketing claim was that productivity would increase and the danger of workplace radicalism could be reduced if firms could quickly and efficiently screen out the maladjusted and miserable. The Woodworth Personal Data Sheet was imitated by a series of competing instruments.[9] The most notable rival, the Bernreuter Personality Inventory (BPI) extended the scope of personality beyond adjustment to include other personality factors.

The testing game was well and truly afoot. And the marketing of these new instruments intensified.

As the BPI established itself as the dominant player in the market, commentators noted the irony in which *the results of so many studies employing the BPI in industrial investigations were negative.* Repeated findings found that the BPI was in fact not doing a good job of predicting employee performance. The dismal results for the BPI opened up an opportunity for better tests. Throughout the 1930s and 40s, a new wave of instruments appeared: the Bell Adjustment Inventory, the Guilford-Martin Personality Inventory of Factors, the Nebraska

Personality Inventory and the Humm-Wadsworth Temperament Scale (HWTS).

In a rerun of the use of the Woodworth Personal Data Sheet, the Humm-Wadsworth Temperament Scale was then taken up to screen neurotic and psychotic soldiers during the drafts of World War 2.

In their review of the history of personality testing, Gibby and Zicker note that much of the success of the HWTS arose from Humm's aggressive tactics in shaping debate about research and validation. *Although it created friction with journal editors and psychologists, these efforts could have been successful in promoting the HWTS as a valid instrument for industry.* This theme - the deployment of robust marketing tactics to advance claims way ahead of the evidence base - would become an established feature for future personality test publishers.

More personality tests followed, notably the MMPI, the 16PF and the Guilford Zimmerman Temperament Survey.

Selecting Spies

Another key development in testing in the mid-20th century was pioneered by the Office of Strategic Studies - the precursor of the CIA - and a rethink of the assessment process for the selection of secret agents.

Following the template of the British War Office Selection Boards, a team of psychologists and psychiatrists worked with the military to set up an assessment centre - Station S - a three day event incorporating a mix of individual and group tasks, exercises requiring improvisation, interviews, projective tests and conventional personality questionnaires, including the Myers Briggs Type Indicator.[10] Between 1943 and 1945, the OSS tested over 5,000 recruits and *evolved as the most complex and time consuming personality check ever made in history.*

Although *validation problems, inherent in all wartime personnel procedures, plagued the programme*, mysteriously for reasons unknown, it was generally viewed by key stakeholders as an improvement on the previous selection system. Importantly the methodology of multiple assessments was to make its way into business, initially as part of a research study, then implemented within the US firm AT & T.

The assessment centre was born and became a standard practice - initially in selection and later in a range of development applications.

Corporate Conformity in the 1950s - 60s

In his 1956 book, The Organization Man, William Whyte observed the rapid take up of personality testing by US corporations. Around 60% of US firms were deploying some kind of personality test or other. He was not impressed. Whyte's argument was that corporate America was going down the wrong path. The pioneering and entrepreneurial spirit of its business leaders was being stifled by conformity and conservatism. Personality testing was one of Whyte's key targets.

Eccentricity has always abounded when and where strength of character has abounded; and the amount of eccentricity in a society has generally been proportional to the amount of genius, mental vigour, and moral courage it contained. **John Stuart Mill, On Liberty**

He was alarmed at how tests were being deployed in selection, and even more concerned by the way in which tests were being used to *check-up* on current employees. Organisations were now looking for the reliable, well-adjusted individual who would fit in and be trusted not to rock the boat. The result: *a set of yardsticks that reward the conformist, the pedestrian, the unimaginative, at the expense of the exceptional individual without whom no organisation can flourish.*

Whyte's argument was that personality testing was doing the opposite of what was claimed. It was eliminating those candidates with distinctive personality. He went on to provide a detailed critique of the tests, their lack of validity and in particular the way in which candidate personality test data was compared with a norm group. For Whyte, this norm is *the result of the instinctive striving of previous test takers to answer as they think everyone else would answer.*

It's inherently sexist to view straightforward women as hostile or rude while approving of men who behave the same way.[11]
Exasperated with the use of shoddy and inappropriate tests badly implemented within selection, Whyte created a cheat sheet with advice to help candidates out-manoeuvre the test publishers. His advice included the guiding principles:

When in doubt about the most beneficial answer to any question, repeat to yourself:

I loved my father and my mother, but my father a little bit more.
I like things pretty much the way they are.
I never worry much about anything.
I don't care for books or music much.
I love my wife and my children.
I don't let them get in the way of company work.

THINGS GET WORSE

In handling a test situation, it is best to make like a grizzly. But be a bear with more growl than incisors. **Martin Gross**

Martin Gross in his 1962 book The Brain Watchers went further in his concerns about personality testing in employee selection. Revisiting the history of personality testing, he questioned the claims of the test publishers.

The Woodworth Personal Data Sheet as applied in the screening of soldiers in World War 1 was a failure. It *did not satisfactorily select the psycho-neurotics from good trench material.* The value of personality testing in military selection in World War 2: *our appraisal of screening in World War 2 points to two conclusions: the screen was not very effective and it had little predictive value.* The Office of Strategic Studies programme for secret agent selection: *none of our statistical computations demonstrates that our system of assessment was of great value.*

Gross also replays George Bennett's summary of the field in the Buros Mental Measurements Yearbook: *Over the past 40 years a great number of self description inventories have been constructed and tried out. This reviewer is unable to recall a well-established instance of useful validity against a criterion of occupational success.*

Noting the boundless enthusiasm for personality testing - *we often don't bother checking references or past experience. We learn more about a person from their personality tests* - Gross reviewed the issues with personality testing, an analysis remarkably prescient of the key issues played out in today's debates.

Badly designed and inappropriately applied tests. Gross reviewed the range of tests, a mix of idiosyncratic instruments derived from a clinical context or psycho-analytical theory as well as more systematic attempts to measure personality, and questioned their relevance to employee selection.

The lack of validation to demonstrate their practical value in selection. Here Gross highlighted that validation claims typically rested on studies with small sample sizes, seldom cross validated, and never replicated in independent research.

Candidate gamesmanship in selection. Like Whyte, Gross argues that the savvy candidate should seek to out-wit the testers. *Keep in mind that you are being statistically compared with a generation of liars before you. Job hunting is hardly the time to upset your career, and the tester's norms, with honest neurotic* *replies.* And adds: *you don't just pass a personality test; you must conquer it.*

The lack of theory to guide how personality shapes work outcomes. Recalling the IBM[12] psychologist - *if it comes out that our best people are all 5 feet 3 with green eyes, it's OK with me -* Gross anticipated the problems with Big Data and predictive analytics that grab correlational patterns without a defensible theory of cause and effect.[13]

The smoke screen of complex statistical methodology. The *adroit use of statistics - numbers that can and do lie - to create an aura of scientific precision that in fact does not exist.* Revisiting the classic *How handsome validity can be distilled from raw nothings by clever maths*[14] Gross highlighted how statistical sorcery can conjure a messy data set into an impressive validity coefficient.

THAT WAS THEN, THIS IS NOW

Yeah, but, no, but, yeah, but, no, but. **Vicki Pollard, Little Britain**

But haven't things moved on since then? The argument from the current generation of test publishers is yes. **Badly designed tests were inappropriately applied**. But we now have access to a range of tests, professionally developed against rigorous psychometric standards. We have shifted away from instruments either designed for clinical use or draw on outdated psychoanalytical thinking, Tests with greater occupational relevance are now deployed.

Validation was problematic. But what would you expect in the early days of a new enterprise? Recent meta-analysis indicate substantial predictive power. The evidence base has been established for personality tests.

The **use of personality tests in selection was largely hit or miss**. But these misguided researchers and practitioners were grappling with a new methodology. We now have sophisticated analytics and decision making models to inform how to weight and integrate personality data into robust formulae to optimise predictive power.

These responses have some merit. What remains puzzling is the ongoing controversy in which:

- **academic researchers** are still unable to agree the value of personality tests in employee selection. Some groups indicate the promise of personality testing in selection. Others argue the evidence base hasn't shifted since the 1960s and the application of personality instruments in high stakes situations can't be justified.
- **publishers and consultants** are engaged in a game of claim and counter-claim about the superiority of their tests vs their rivals, but with little supporting evidence.
- **practitioners** remain confused in their evaluation of personality tests and which tests to use and how test data should be integrated with other assessments in selection.

Resolving the Puzzle of Personality Testing

I have almost never broken off a friendship. ***True or False***

The apparent breakthrough findings of the 1990s[15] have, with further analysis, turned out to be highly fragile. Kevin Murphy makes the point: *empirical support for the use of personality measures in organisational settings has changed very little since the Guion and Gottier review of 1965.*[16] And that *validity estimates for personality measures are often distressingly close to zero.*

Any number of innovations in psychometric methodology, insights into personality's impact in the work-place and the impact of on line technology should have delivered significant predictive gains. And given personality's well established association with a range of significant life outcomes[17] the limitations of self report personality tests in selection are remarkable. Why?

Measures of broad personality dimensions show levels of validity in predicting performance but rarely all that far from zero. **Kevin Murphy**

Five themes are outlined:

- problems within the validation research; predictive validity is a game of **statistical smoke and mirrors**.

- the realities of **self deception** and its impact in self report measures.

- how **faking** in applicant scenarios operates and its impact in selection decision making.

- the **lack of theory** to connect personality to performance; how the interplay of context, cause and consequence makes prediction difficult.

- the hazards of integrating personality test data within **selection decision making** and how best to combine the intuition of expert judgement with predictive algorithms.

Is validity no longer valid?

Validity as face validity - it looks like it should work - in personality testing is easy, both in questionnaire completion for candidates as well as in the report back of the results. The Forer effect comes to the rescue to ensure that candidates will for the most part happily agree with their profiles.[18]

Disciplined and self-controlled outside, you tend to be worrisome and insecure inside. At times you have serious doubts as to whether you have made the right decision or done the right thing. You prefer a certain amount of change and variety and become dissatisfied when hemmed in by restrictions and limitations. **Bertram Forer**

This finding was observed in a further study. Instead of giving individuals their *true* results, the experimenter handed out a trumped up personality analysis report composed of statements lifted from astrology charts. Asked to evaluate the test's validity, nine out of ten agreed their reports were good or amazingly accurate descriptions of their personality.

Test validation - methodological design, sampling and the interpretation of the findings - is complex. Part of the confusion in the debate for the James Randi Psychometric Award lay in the use of the word **prediction**.

How the test publishers use the prediction word is very different to the practitioner expectation. For the practitioner, quite reasonably, a prediction means that a forecast in Time 1 is observed as an outcome in Time 2. There is no expectation of 100% accuracy; only an anticipation that the probabilities have shifted sufficiently to improve predictive power. How predictable something is depends on: what we are trying to predict, how far into the future and under what circumstances. Most test publishers interpret prediction very differently. Overviewing the evidence base for personality test validity, a few summary points can be made:

Validity coefficients **tend to be higher for personality tests when reported by publishers than by academic researchers**. This may be an issue of sample sizes. It may also be the result of cherry picking positive studies for publication, and putting negative findings in the file drawer.[19] The manuals of the test publisher to indicate the validity of personality assessment are unrepresentative of the broader set of research findings. As Frank Schmidt observed: *it is no accident that psychologists associated with the test publishers display the most conviction about the value of personality testing in employee selection.*

Real evidence is usually vague and unsatisfactory. It has to be examined---sifted. But here the whole thing is cut and dried. No, my friend, this evidence has been very cleverly manufactured - so cleverly that it has defeated its own ends. **Agatha Christie**

Validity studies are overwhelmingly based on **a concurrent design**. This research draws on current incumbents, employees already selected and in role. Rarely do validation studies utilise a controlled trial where applicant test data - not used in selection - tracks performance over time.

For the test publishers, prediction is largely assumed from a correlation between personality test data and work performance both observed in Time 1. Given that incumbents represent a different sample group to applicants this makes the claim of predictive power problematic in real life selection. Results from a concurrent research design cannot be assumed to generalise to predictive gains in the high stakes scenario of selection.

Concurrent studies also **confound cause and consequence**. Self-confidence, for example, is found to be a correlate of current performance for a sales group. Eager practitioners now factor this finding into their assessment systems and selection decision making models. But it is more likely that self-confidence is an outcome of higher sales today than a predictive input of sales effectiveness tomorrow.[20]

Most validity studies **use supervisory ratings as the criterion of work performance.** This is understandable. These appraisals are accessible and inexpensive to collect. This validation enterprise however hinges on evaluations the test publishers previously dismissed as highly subjective and inadequate metrics of performance.

This opens up a paradox. On the one hand, the test publishers say that objective testing is required because managers are hopeless in recruitment interviews, performance appraisal, and talent reviews. On the other hand, the metric for validation is based on the evaluations the psychometricians criticised in the first place. When validity is established by drawing on these flawed criteria, by what logic is validity demonstrated?[21]

OUTSTANDING PROBLEMS

Statistical Smoke And Mirrors

SC Wave is the perfect tool to help predict workplace performance/potential. It predicts overall job proficiency at 0.38, and promotability at 0.59.

A typical job interview has a 1% correlation between what you see in an interview and actual job skills. Using ESP raises your predictability value to 60-70%.[22]

This is personality assessment that has gone down the rabbit hole of Alice in Wonderland.

Test publishers typically indicate the value of their instruments with a correlation coefficient (r), an index to indicate the size and direction of a relationship, from -1 to +1. A zero relationship means there is no relationship between a personality test score and whichever success criterion is being utilised, through to 1, a perfect correlation. Interpreting these correlation coefficients is a confusing enterprise. Kevin Murphy argues: *personality researchers and practitioners seem to have lost track of just what it means for a test to be valid.*

Meta-analysis is the methodology to consolidate hundreds of different validation studies, a procedure intended to iron out the statistical wrinkles and correct for various anomalies, sample sizes, restriction of change and more, from all the vagaries of different research designs. In the case of assessment, these meta-analytical studies collate the evidence for the validity of different methods. Validity is intended to provide confidence. The higher the validity, the more certain practitioners can be in the assessments they apply. This exercise is helpful as a high level summary of the kind of predictive power that might be expected in **principle**. These coefficients do not determine in **practice** what predictive power will be achieved in a given selection context.

The U.S. psychometrician Wendall Williams makes the point: *a statistical meta-analysis can suggest: by golly, it might work. But that is a far cry from proclaiming it actually does work.*

The Problem of Validity Generalisation

The psychometricians report the conclusions from meta-analytical studies and assume the validity of an assessment method can be generalised. Practitioners have assurance that a specific method will be valid across different selection scenario for a range of roles, levels and industries.

It was validity generalisation in the 1980s that restored the credibility of previously derided measures of general mental ability (GMA). Here there was compelling evidence that for pretty much any role, GMA would be a useful predictor. In a recent round-up of the evidence, Frank Schmidt[23] confirms that GMA remains one of the most consistent and cost effective predictors of work place performance.

The personality test publishers were quick to jump on the band-wagon of validity generalisation.[24] A personality test that can be trusted to work *any time, any place, anywhere* is a test for acceptance in the market place. Unlike mental ability this appeal to generalisation proved troublesome. Personality test validity does not in fact transport easily to different organisational cultures or roles.[25]

Even more challenging for the practitioner is the fragility of the results reported by the meta-analytical researchers - at least for some assessment methods. Conscientiousness, for example, one of the brightest personality stars in the validity firmament, with most predictive promise, was reported with a validity coefficient of 0.31 in the late 1990s, then as 0.22 in 2016. And in a 2023 review as 0.19.[26] Here it is tempting to recall the scene from the BBC docu-sitcom, The Thick Of It. Spin doctor Malcolm Tucker explains how advisers work:

My expert would totally disprove that.

Who is your expert?

I don't know, but I can get one by this afternoon. The thing is, you've been listening to the wrong expert. You need to listen to the right expert. And you need to know what an expert is going to advise you before he advises you.[27]

What has been forgotten is that validity is not an intrinsic property of a personality test. Validity operates within a context. It indicates the strength of the inferences that can be drawn from the use of a test within a specific selection scenario. Without an understanding of the base rate of current effectiveness and the selection ratio in recruitment, generalised claims of incremental predictive gains are misleading.

You can't fix by meta-analysis what investigators bungled by design. **Professor James Coyne**

Life would be so much simpler if the test publishers moved away from the abstraction of the correlation coefficient. These statistics are largely an exercise in flag waving - *my test is better than your test* - but lack meaning for practitioners in the specific selection context they face.

When the assessment consultant opens their validity kimono to reveal a 0.5 correlation, ask for a scatter plot. *What data patterns lie behind a correlation coefficient?* **Jan Vanhove**[28]

The recommendation is to shift towards the kind of predictive meaning provided by natural frequencies[29], expectancy tables or scatter-plots. Or, even better to follow the lead of the bookmakers when they offer the odds of success. Perhaps the easiest metric for validation in personality testing is the Ronseal test: *it does exactly what it says on the tin*. What is the specific claim and does the evidence deliver on this claim?

Many have thought that the bigger and more ambiguous the promise, the bigger the payoff. It is usually the opposite. The more specific the promise, the more salient the proposition. **Advertising guru, Bob Hoffman**

Self Deception: Who Is Kidding Who?

I am a very stable genius. **Former US President Donald Trump**

For the personality testers, candidates in employee selection possess full self awareness of themselves and their personality. In this ideal world of the publishers, candidates are also motivated to disclose fully this information about themselves to recruiters. We do not operate in this ideal world. The first challenge is that self evaluation is a difficult task. Here the evidence base is fairly robust.[30]

We are not very good at judging with accuracy our own competence and character.

People on average tend to believe themselves to be above average on positive qualities. And on average, to report themselves below average on negative qualities. To compound the problem, individuals also believe they are more likely than their peers to provide accurate self assessments.

There are different dynamics at play. Self awareness is uncomfortable. As Goethe said: *Know thyself? If I knew myself, I'd run away.* We also lack key information to arrive at an accurate evaluation of ourselves. Feedback that might improve accuracy is often difficult to recognise, biased and subject to misinterpretation.

Don't accept your dog's admiration as conclusive evidence that you are wonderful. **Ann Landers**

At one level, accuracy in self evaluation should have many benefits. Clear thinking about our strengths allows us to optimise our impact. A knowledge of our shortcomings helps avoid those situations that might expose our weaknesses, weaknesses that if played out, heighten the likelihood of failure.

Alternatively, as evolutionary psychology suggests, self insight is unlikely to be a straightforward process. A lack of self insight may in fact be important in the game of survival and success. *If we can lie to ourselves, it helps us lie to others more convincingly.*[31] If self insight is an issue for everyone, the problem is compounded by the much publicised Dunning-Kruger Effect.[32]

People who lack the knowledge or wisdom to perform well are often unaware of this fact. We attribute this lack of awareness to a deficit in metacognitive skill. That is, the same incompetence that leads them to make wrong choices also deprives them of the savvy necessary to recognize competence, be it their own or anyone else's.

Here the most self insightful individuals report relatively lower competence than the less insightful individuals who claim superior competence. Self deception is no trivial issue, particularly at senior leadership levels. *Over-confidence in CEOs, for example, results in the hubris that underpins disastrous mergers and acquisitions.*[33]

And it represents a significant hazard in self report measures. If self awareness is one element of emotional intelligence, it is difficult to identify the psychological process in which individuals who are low in self awareness manage to report themselves as low in emotional intelligence.

In one research programme, the top ten endorsed personality items emerged as:

I like to read; visit new places; was a better than average student when I was in school; am a good listener; would love to explore strange places; am concerned about others; am open to new experiences; amuse my friends; love excitement; spend a lot of time reading.[34]

An encouraging and wonderful insight into human personality. We seem to be open minded intellectuals, empathic and understanding, and exciting and amusing company. Alternatively, *most of us are not really very good at evaluating where we stand in relation to other people, at least for many traits.*

Tal Yarkoni

If You Can't Make It, Just Fake It

I'm not really makin' it. This feeling of fakin' it. I still haven't shaken it. **Paul Simon and Art Garfunkel**

If self deception addresses the relative inability to complete a personality test in which our subjective perceptions correspond to objective reality, impression management is the motivation to project a positive image to others.

As with market research, the problem is *that people don't think what they feel, they don't say what they think, and they don't do what they say.* **Rory Sutherland**

We can describe the intentional attempt to distort responses in personality test completion as impression management. Alternatively, we can call it faking, estimated to occur with at least between 30 to 40% of applicants.[35]

In light of our knowledge regarding deception, the research question of do applicants fake? is silly. The better question might be: Why wouldn't they fake? **R Griffith and M McDaniel**

While over 70% of practitioners view faking as a challenge within employee selection, researchers and test publishers are divided about its impact in recruitment decision making. The arguments run:

Faking is not an issue. The argument here is, yes, faking does occur, but it doesn't appreciably affect the reliability and validity of personality testing in selection. This is the stance of *nothing to view here. Move on*. Intuitively, faking might be expected to undermine the value of personality testing in high stakes selection scenarios. Empirically, it doesn't seem to make that much difference.[36]

The corporate person is adjusted to the needs of the present. The time will come as it always has when people will need new concepts and when crises now unheard of will have to be faced. The premium then will be on the force of the individual personality and an impatience with complacent schemes of social stupidity. **Andrew Hacker**

Faking is a good thing. This position is that of course impression management occurs[37] and this is a positive. It is part of the social game in which the savvy candidate gets it, and the guileless don't. After all, the ability to understand and play this game is an important predictor of future performance.[38] This results in the bizarre conclusion from the advocates of faking good that *sometimes telling the literal truth invalidates the assessment process.*

This is an untenable position. The projection of a best self may be an indicator of social competence for some roles. But if the

39

claim is that the validity of a personality test hinges on who can best fake, we move into turbulent professional and ethical waters. The expectation that *peoples' responses to personality test items will create the same impression that their behaviour creates in real life* is extremely optimistic. There is little evidence to indicate that successful fakers will also fake good in the work place. Even worse, organisations encounter the successful faking of the sociopathic candidate.[39]

In a time of declining organisational trust, the typical admonition - *there are no right or wrong answers. Please complete honestly* - is a sham that can only contribute further to employee cynicism. One test publisher provides the advice: *Rule 1: when taking a personality test - be yourself.*[40] This is not helpful advice if your results are going to be compared with *a generation of liars before you.* The applicant perception - informed by social media exchanges of how to pass the personality test - is that:

You play a game.
I know you play this game.
And you know that I know how to play this game.
And that's how the game will work in future for me to succeed as an employee.

The best tests assume that people will lie and fake and take that into account, because faking is a sign of competence. **Tomas Chamorro-Premuzic, Chief Talent Scientist, Manpower Group**

It does nothing for employee trust. In the category of stuff you can't make up, the keenest advocates of the proposal that faking is a good thing - with unembarrassable chutzpah - point to alarming rates of management failure.[41] There is another explanation for management failure.[42] Faking is part of the game as an applicant, recruiter, as an employee and a manager. And levels of organisational trust have fallen.

The third stance is that **faking is a major problem** in employee selection but it can be minimised. This is the challenge facing practitioners in personnel selection. The research base points to significant hazards of faking within personality testing in selection:

- most personality measures can be faked fairly easily.
- a significant number of applicants do fake; *42% of respondents report they had given false impressions of themselves in the completion of personality tests.*
- 74% of applicants believe that other applicants engage in faking activity.

- different applicants employ different faking strategies and adopt different tactics from extreme faking to modest faking.
- attempts to detect faking are ineffective and may be counter-productive.
- applicant samples produce lower validity coefficients than incumbent samples.[43]
- faking affects who does and doesn't gets hired.[44]

Given the extent of the problem, what are the typical responses to faking? Despite the *nothing to see here, move on* argument of a minority of researchers, the majority in the field are concerned. Substantial research has been committed to identify the strategies that will minimise its prevalence, detect its presence and mitigate its impact.

Preventing faking

The most common strategy is the use of warning messages. *Do NOT click through the SHL Occupational Personality Questionnaire randomly or try to distort it in some way; it is built the way that it shows up on the results and you may be disqualified from further assessment process; remember there are no right or wrong answers in this test; the purpose is to find the best fit candidates.*[45]

This rather incoherent message implies that faking behaviour can be spotted. The ethics are problematic given the reality that faking cannot be detected easily. Another paradox emerges: highly rule conscious applicants heed the warnings while those low on rule conscious ignore the message. The outcome for the end user: low rule conscious candidates are profiled as higher on Conscientiousness than those higher on rule conscious.

Inclusion of **bogus statements** within the questionnaire. Applicants are asked to report their knowledge or experience of non-existent items, for example, of made up authors or nonsensical scientific terminology. When applicants respond in the affirmative, the logic is that they are over claiming and attempting to project an overly positive impression of themselves. This is another highly compromised design strategy. The conclusion is that more research is needed. Of course. But more fundamental ethical issues need to be resolved if lying is needed to identify liars.

The dirty little secret of the polygraph is that it depends on trickery, not science. If the lie detector does work, it only works by virtue of the fact that some people think it works because they are fooled by the deceptions of the tester to convince individuals that the test is infallible. A typical trick in the use of the polygraph. Individuals undergoing the lie detector are asked to select a playing card from a deck and asked a series of questions about their selected card while their responses are monitored by the lie detector, and are astounded by the responses from the lie detector - unaware that all the cards in the deck are identical.[46]

Covert rather than overt personality test items. The shift in the 1980s and 1990s towards greater occupational relevance in the design of personality tests for employee selection had the virtue of transparency. But it came with a vice: obvious content that was easily fakeable within employee selection. Compare two types of personality test items:

I like the feel of furry silk lined slippers, taken from the Grygier Dynamic Personality Inventory versus *I am highly conscientious*, a typical item from a mainstream popular test.
Which is more or less fakeable?

Overt items are the personality statements that are clear to candidates. They immediately understand what the statement is intended to measure. Covert items are less clear to the candidate and make it more difficult to work out what is being assessed. And there are indications that covert items are less susceptible to faking.[47] A psychometric balance needs to be struck in the construction of personality tests. This design philosophy steers clear of those statements that are so obvious in their intent they encourage faking. It also avoids items that incorporate such subtlety or express odd activities they lack face validity or intrude into the personal lives of applicants.

An example. A personality test item from a well-known personality instrument: *As a child, people said I was cute.* Does this work? Probably not; this seems highly questionable for several reasons.

Arguably, the shift towards greater occupational relevance in test design has compounded the problem and tilted the balance toward greater fakeability. Predictive validity for organisational impact has been lost in the need for the face validity of reassuring blandness and commercial return.[48]

Detecting faking

Social desirability response scales; their usage should be discontinued. **Delroy Paulhus**

Response distortion scales, typically known as Lie or Social Desirability Response (SDR) scales, have been used extensively in personality measures. Around 85% of popular personality tests deploy some variation of these scales. The aim is to *trap dishonest respondents in their deception. Would you ever lie to people?*

Social Desirability Response scales consist of unlikely statements along the lines of *I always keep my promises* or *I never tell a lie*. The assumption: when highly positive statements are endorsed, and negative statements are not endorsed, the candidate has faked the rest of the personality test. The give away for the savvy game playing candidate is in the frequency qualifiers.

The research indicates a number of hazards with this approach. Firstly, the scales themselves tend to be **easily fakeable**. High SDR scores confuse intentional faking with the naïve candidate who is unable to rumble the racket, but *blessed with an abundance of socially desirable attributes.* Another confounding factor is the candidate interpretation of the statements that make up the scales. Faking gets mixed up with the extent to which some candidates are literal minded and rightly refuse to endorse any never or always statements[49] versus those candidates who go with the flow of the sentiment behind the statement.

Secondly, different **SDR scales do not correlate well**. *Different detectors of faking result in different classifications of respondents. Whether an individual is classified as having faked does not necessarily depend on their actual faking behaviour but on the method utilised for detection.* When the validity of scales designed to detect faking is low, it is difficult to justify their usage.

In one bizarre consulting assignment, an assessment exercise was implemented as part of an organisational restructure, a mix of external recruitment and the redeployment of current professionals and managers. Almost 80% of the 250 candidates scored highly on a Social Desirability Response scale.

When challenged, the test publisher of a widely used personality test from a global consulting firm agreed - only after much reluctance - to meet to work through the puzzle of this response pattern. As it turned out, there was a problem with the scoring and normative protocols. Red faces all round at the test publisher, and much embarrassment to recover a selection fiasco.

Third, high SDR scores are also **associated with the traits associated with work performance.**

Asked to rate how sensible they are, sensible people give themselves a 7 or 8. 9 or 10 wouldn't be sensible. **Guy Browning**

Even if Social Desirability Response scales did work, the practical issue is then how candidate scores are deployed in selection. The options:

- remove high scoring SDR candidates from the applicant pool.

- apply some correction formula to recalibrate the personality test data.
- ask high scoring SDR candidates to recomplete with the implication that the first completion was a dishonest response.

None of these strategies seem defensible.[50]

The **removal of high SDR candidates** has a negligible effect on both criterion-related validity and job performance. Adjustments for high SDR scores appear to make little difference. The retesting of candidates may make a modest difference. Practically it may be difficult to implement, and not without ethical and legal consequences. Non faking candidates who do register high on SDR scales - the false positives - may resent the accusation of deception and seek legal redress if they are unsuccessful in selection.[51]

In the latest systematic review of the research[52] the conclusion is: *the use of social desirability scales to index faking behaviour is inaccurate, and the use of social desirability scales to correct personality scores may do more harm than good.*

Forced choice design

In the 1980 - 90s, personality test designers found themselves between the rock of occupational relevance but transparent fakeability and the hard place of non-obvious subtlety but indefensible face validity.

Various formats and response tasks and anchors were explored to replace the standard response scale - typically from strongly disagree to strongly agree - to overcome the problem of these test taking liars.

An item from a well-known personality assessment: *I have almost never broken off a friendship*. True or False? Yes or No? Is this a better alternative to a 1 - 5 rating scale?[53] Probably not. This baffling question seems a test of verbal critical reasoning. Or possibly a measure of telepathy to work out the intention of a test designer with bad grammar.

Do frequency scales provide more rigour? Probably not.

ALVY'S PSYCHIATRIST: How often do you sleep together?
ALVY: Hardly ever. Maybe three times a week.
ANNIE'S PSYCHIATRIST: Do you have sex often?
ANNIE: Constantly! I'd say three times a week.[54]

Forced choice measurement was seen as a way for the fly to escape from the bottle of faking. Forced choice formats come in different shapes and sizes. Typically candidates are presented with pairs, trios or quartets of statements matched for social desirability or undesirability. And required to select the statement that is more or less descriptive of them. The logic is that since candidates cannot select all the positive statements or avoid all the negative statements, forced choice tests should be less susceptible to faking.

For savvy candidates, test taking moves up a level in the game. Not only do they need to keep their SDR scores low, they also need to work out which statements to rank given their insight into the traits of most job relevance.

Overlooked in this shift towards ipsative forced choice formats for personality testing was the impact on conventional psychometric statistics, measurement properties and the interpretation of validation findings. Also forgotten was the questionable assumption that ipsative test data can be treated as equivalent to candidate scores as obtained from the typical rating response task.

A market research scenario. Two respondents complete a questionnaire about drink preferences. The format presents a series of four drink types and respondents are asked to select their most and least preferred drink of choice. In, for example, quartet one:

Vodka, Whisky, Gin, Rum

Respondent 1 is a near teetotaller who drinks extremely rarely. They select rum as most and whisky as their least preferred drink. Respondent 2 is an almost alcoholic whose daily intake of whatever is available is extremely high. This individual selects: vodka as most and rum as their least preferred choice. In the world of forced choice testing that introduces normative comparison, the conclusion would be that the near teetotaller drinks rum more than the almost alcoholic. [55]

But the downsides of ipsative forced choice instruments - problematic psychometric properties and the hazards of candidate comparison - could just about be justified if faking is prevented and genuine predictive gains are demonstrated.

Have forced choice designs mitigated the faking problem?
The jury remains out. Different research and practitioner groups report conflicting findings. In one summary of the evidence base: *the empirical literature has not produced persuasive evidence for the elimination of faking amongst highly motivated test takers when forced choice formats are used.*[56] It is not obvious what predictive gains have been achieved.

The suggestion is that any improvements in validity are less about the personality of candidates than their level of general mental ability. The conclusion seems to be that any modest predictive gains in selection are largely the result of candidate cognitive skills to work out the necessary response pattern for the role. Not what was intended.

The chief cause of problems is solutions. **Sevareid's Law**

The research on faking and its impact within employee selection can be summarised:

Faking Performance = Opportunity X Motivation X Ability

Opportunity is based on a combination of the transparency of the personality test and the obviousness of any Social Desirability Response scale that is used to detect faking. When questionnaire content is apparent and the SDR scale items lack subtlety, we can anticipate successful undetected faking. In a scenario where a personality inventory has finesse and nuance in item content and response format, greater honesty can be expected.

Motivation is shaped by the purpose of the personality test. When results are confidential to the individual and utilised as part of a personal development application, we can assume that faking will be less frequent than in the high stakes scenario of employee selection.

The **Ability** to fake is complicated. In "The g in Faking"[57] the evidence indicates that intelligence predicts successful faking ability. The implication is that any incremental validity of personality testing in forced choice formats is due to cognitive aptitude rather than any variance in personality.

Any defensible method to detect faking must meet three criteria:

- Have a **high detection rate** and avoid false positives. As McCrae and Costa highlight: *Paradoxically it is the most honest and upstanding citizen that these scales would lead us to accuse of lying.* When the frequency of false positives is higher than the true positives, there is a selection problem. There is also a major ethical difficulty.
- Scores **should not capture relevant trait variance and eliminate top candidates**. Given that emotional stability, agreeableness and conscientiousness correlate with SDR scores, traits often associated with work performance, the risk is that highly suitable candidates will be ruled out of the selection game.
- The method should **not be coachable** to allow applicants to spot the detection tactic in a selection situation. In the world of social media and the many guidelines on how to fake the test, this is unlikely.

No method meets these three criteria.

Much like the mythical unicorn, a solution to the faking problem in personality testing has been an exciting but elusive quarry.
Michael Zikar and Katherine Sliter

The Missing Theory

What we can say with confidence is that personality is a more complex and versatile phenomenon than is reflected in a personality test score. **Luke Smillie**[58]

Levels of Personality

The personality testing industry has been dominated by trait theory. Having overcome the situationalist critique of the 1960s and 70s,[59] the trait enterprise in the 1980s rediscovered its mojo to develop a range of new personality tests. More recently, several publishers have integrated competency based approaches with the trait perspective to include, for example, the dimensions of persuasion and innovation. This test design strategy seems to have built instruments that are now self report measures of ability. The problems of self deception and impression management have been compounded.

The trait approach assumes that as individuals we have deep seated temperamental dispositions that shape in important ways what we do and how we do it. These traits are played out in significant life outcomes.[60]

There remains debate however about the best way to map out these personality traits. The Big 5 model of OCEAN: Openness,

Conscientiousness, Extraversion, Agreeableness and Neuroticism, at one point seemed to have achieved reasonable consensus amongst researchers. But this has been recently challenged.[61] The Big Five may be problematic across different cultures, income levels, educational achievements and age groups.[62]

The Big Five makes me think of being in a spaceship, looking down at the planet below and seeing five continents. That's useful to know, but once you're back on earth it won't help you find your way home. **Annie Murphy Paul**

There is the suggestion that an additional sixth factor of honesty/humility might provide a better alternative.[63] Or even more remarkably, there is only one single personality dimension as a kind of *p factor,* equivalent to the *g factor* in the ability domain.[64]

The fundamental problem goes unaddressed by most test publishers. The assumption that traits can describe personality adequately is flawed. Dan McAdams[65] makes the point that traits represent only one level of personality.

A good trait analysis would appear to be little more than a systematic psychology of the stranger. **Dan McAdams**

At the first level, **traits** represent a starting point to think about personality. Some people are generally more or less agreeable or assertive. For others extraversion or their introversion is an important factor underpinning behaviour, and so on. This helps us make some sense of others.

The second level McAdams calls **characteristic adaptations**. This reflect others' personal concerns, how they define themselves with reference to the roles they play, the skills they value, the interests that make them passionate, and the goals they have for the future. We now move to a much deeper understanding of the individual and what makes them tick.

The third level is to understand the **life story** that individuals construct to connect their past, present and anticipated future. This is how individuals make sense of their lives. At this level we gain a profounder insight into others' fears and concerns, priorities and pressures, aspirations and dreams. Personality becomes the strategies used to navigate through these challenges, the opportunities to seize and threats to overcome. A much more textured perspective, this is personality as the individual as a story tellers of their lives.

Once you label me, you negate me. **Søren Kierkegaard**

If personality tests have limited explanatory and predictive power, it may be because most assessments have been designed at the level of dispositional traits, and do not reflect the complexity and range of individual psychology.

Measuring Performance

There are things that can be measured. There are things that are worth measuring. But what can be measured is not always what is worth measuring; what gets measured may have no relationship to what we really want to know. **Jerry Muller, The Tyranny of Metrics**

If personality - how it is best conceptualised and measured - is still in dispute, the challenge is compounded by the issues of performance evaluation.[66] If we can't agree on the criteria of performance and what is being predicted in the first place, it seems difficult to know where to start in the construction of assessment predictors.

Here the question is: **what constitutes job performance?**

I spent a lot of money on booze, birds and fast cars. The rest I just squandered. **George Best, voted the fifth best football player of all time**

Michael Raynor makes the point that the business success genre often looks in the wrong place for genuine metrics of performance.[67] If this is true at an organisational level, it seems particularly applicable for individual performance. Even more awkward: there is reason to believe that some organisations positively reward bad behaviour.[68]

From a validation study of a widely used measure of dark side leadership.

Based on prior theory and the experiences of practitioners, we hypothesized negative relationships between the subclinical disorders and leader development over time. With regard to this hypothesis, our results were certainly more ambivalent. .....we found positive relationships with leader development over time and across multiple dimensions of leadership. The remaining dimensions had few or inconsistent effects. The results require some explanation.[69]

They certainly do. Here we find ourselves meeting Alice in Wonderland again. Are personality tests now predicting the opposite of what firms hope to achieve?

Much greater care was being given to the development of predictors than to the criterion measures against which they were being validated. **Linda Gottfredson**

The standard go to criterion of work performance has been supervisory ratings. As discussed, this is problematic.

The British Psychological Society, by allowing validation studies based on the equivalent of nine ladies dancing and ten lords a-leaping as evidence of practical value, green lighted test publishers to claim BPS endorsement in their marketing.[70]

When line management ratings of individual effectiveness correlate only modestly with those of an individual's peers and team members, who is providing the most accurate feedback of performance? If success is in the eye of the beholder, which beholder determines who is and is not effective? What do we do when validation studies report different findings against these very different evaluations?

The solution to the subjectivity and low validity of line management evaluations has been the search for objective performance metrics. For many roles this has been relatively straightforward. Data about sales, service responsiveness and productivity, etc. can be accessed across a spectrum of jobs. More problematic has been the measurement of innovation.[71]

Objective metrics have their own hazards. When, for example, a surgeon's performance is evaluated and rewarded against patient survival rates, an improvement could be anticipated in overall mortality rates. Not necessarily when surgeons game the system by choosing to operate only on those patients they know have a higher chance of survival and discriminate against those patients they don't think will make it through surgery.

The success rates of the high performing surgeons are relatively lower vis a vis their peers in other hospitals **because** of their success. Here health outcomes are distorted. And validation findings are highly misleading. Which metrics should we use to evaluate nursing teams? Are error rates an indicator of an under-performing team? Paradoxically, nursing teams with better team leader-nurse relationships report more errors. These teams have the confidence - unlike the less effective teams - to acknowledge any mistakes and review the reasons for future improvements.

In The Tyranny of the Metrics, Jerry Muller points to the many perverse incentives and negative unintended consequences associated with the introduction of quantifiable measures of performance. For many roles objective performance metrics cannot be accessed with any confidence.

Count no one a success until the end is known. **Solon**

When Fred Goodwin was selected as Forbes Global's Business Leader of the Year in 2002, was he an excellent CEO? Or, a dismal performer when the Royal Bank of Scotland collapsed six years later, triggering a government bailout to the tune of £45 billion? Was Jack Welch the greatest business leader of the 20th century as announced by Fortune magazine? Or an exploitative leader whose focus on delivering short term earnings brought about the fall of the house of GE?[72]

Measure what you can, evaluate what you measure, and appreciate that you cannot measure the vast majority of what you do. **Ed Catmull, President of Pixar**

If the response is that we cannot in many instances differentiate low and high performers to evaluate relative business contribution, personality performance theory is extremely fragile.

The Personality Performance Linkage

When the data on the correlation between two variables revealed only a shapeless cloud, he would simply place a pair of meaty hands on the offending bits of the cloud and reveal the straight line hiding from conventional mathematics. **Matthew Stewart, The Management Myth**

The assumption is that specific attributes of personality increase the likelihood of the behaviours associated with greater effectiveness in the tasks that impact on the outcomes of importance to the organisation. It is proving difficult however to identify any straightforward dynamic between personality inputs and performance outputs across a range of roles.

Achievement involves a complex interaction of many personal and environmental variables that feed off each other in non-linear, mutually reinforcing, and nuanced ways, and that the most complete understanding of the development of performance can only be arrived through an integration of perspectives. **Scott Barry Kaufman**

There is any interplay of moderating and mediating factors at work:

- **Context**: the permutations of strategy, structure and culture that set the environment for expectations and levels of performance.
- **Causal** factors: the interactions of experience, cognitive aptitude, motivation and personality and how they combine for different performance outcomes.
- **Consequence**: the different drivers of short vs long-term metrics of task and situational outcomes.

Context, cause and consequence are proving extremely difficult to disentangle in personality testing.

Any number multiplied by zero, no matter how large the number, is still zero. **Charlie Munger**

The practitioner who assumes a tidy linear one-directional causal effect between personality and performance will be disappointed. Although general mental ability largely operates in a simple way: more input = more output, there is no reason to believe this is the case for personality attributes. Instead there are any number of interactive effects. For example, extraversion may lead to higher levels of performance for conscientious employees. But extraversion is associated with lower performance when conscientiousness levels are low.[73]

To add to the complexity, Stephen Woods[74] points to the evidence that it is not simply a case of personality impacting on performance. Work outcomes also shape the development of personality traits. This research insight shifts the debate to explore how work place performance also impacts on employee personality and its development.

Chockalingam Viswesvaran and Deniz Ones rightly say: *the concept of validation would collapse to a futile exercise if the criterion measures were idiosyncratic to particular raters or specific alternate indices of performance.* In the case of personality testing, this is exactly the problem. Validation collapses when the criterion measures are unreliable and fail to explain how personality variation results in performance outcomes.

A good theory to connect personality to performance ideally combines:

- **Simplicity** and ease of understanding. We get it quickly.
- **Accuracy** to work in explaining and predicting events of consequence.
- **Generalisabilit**y that can be applied across a broad range of situations.

The theory to connect the context, causes and consequences of the personality-performance nexus meets none of these criteria. Instead, the linkages between personality and performance are:

- highly **complex**, involving any number of mediating and moderating factors and their interactions.
- **imprecise** in making future predictions of work performance.
- highly **specific** to the context in which personality affects performance outcomes.

The test publishing industry continues to claim personality predicts future performance within pretty much any selection scenario. This is highly implausible, and given recent shifts in employment patterns - a greater emphasis on team collaboration, flexible working, the application of AI functionality - one that is increasingly indefensible.

There is nothing more practical than a good theory. **James Clerk Maxwell**

If self report personality testing is to establish its credibility as a valuable approach in employee selection, a rethink of the interplay of context, cause and consequence is needed. As it stands, personality testing in employment selection lacks a good theory.

Stall Within Selection Decision Making

To explain the past we need complex rules. To predict the future, less is more. **Gerd Gigerenzer**

A thought experiment

For one moment, we put aside concerns about self deception and impression management in personality test completion. We also forget the complexities of validity and the messiness of the current evidence base. And we ignore the challenges of linking personality inputs to performance outputs. Instead, in this thought experiment we imagine that personality has become an established predictor of performance. **How practically should personality test data be utilised in selection decision making?**

Different models can be applied, spanning the spectrum from the holistic and intuitive to the empirical and algorithmic.

Holistic and Intuitive

Historically, the most common approach to personality tests in selection has been informal.

A profile is used to inform interview priorities and coverage to explore how the candidate's personality may shape their work approach and performance.

This analysis is interpreted by the assessor[75] to feed into a selection recommendation and decision. Judgement is applied to integrate the results from the personality test with other assessment data to build a better understanding of the candidate.[76]

This seems a low risk strategy. But one with a caveat. As Steve Blinkhorn pointed out: *As a candidate I would rather complete a bad assessment and be interviewed by a good assessor, rather than undertake a good assessment with a bad assessor.*

This is wise counsel. It takes us back however to the Forer Effect in which any randomised profile might do the trick with a decent interviewer. This area has been neglected; there is little research to indicate the incremental gains of an interview with or without access to personality profiles, randomised or not. This is hardly the stuff of predictive power.[77]

There is also reason to think that confirmation bias influences the recruiter. When results from personality profiling align with interviewer judgements they are acknowledged. When however a personality assessment disagrees with interviewer perceptions, the test data is ignored. This is personality testing as a signal to indicate objectivity in the selection process.[78] If candidates look to manage impressions in selection, then organisations also want to project a positive image of systematic rigour - even if the results of personality profiling are largely disregarded by recruiting interviewers.

In a variation of this informal strategy, some organisations argue that whilst the results from the personality profiling may not affect the selection decision, they are still useful when reviewed with successful candidates as part of their induction. The objective is to identify any potential strengths or shortcomings to help employees get up to speed in their first six months. A progressive approach to help the transition, in principle this has virtue. In practice it rarely happens. Mostly personality data during the application process disappears into a black hole.

There is also the contentious issue of shelf life; how long should personality data be retained on employee personnel files? One site suggests: *When it comes to personality assessments, results are typically valid for a range between 12 months and two years.*[79] It is difficult to know what this recommendation means, never mind find any empirical support for this advice.

Ideal Profile

Further up the spectrum from the intuitive to the empirical is the mapping of the optimal personality. In this strategy, a profile is created to target those dimensions that are seen as key to success for a specific role. Assume, for example, that super-productive software developers share specific personality characteristics. This should provide important insights to assess the suitability of candidates for a software developer role. The challenge: how to create this ideal software developer profile? Software developers come in any variety of shapes and sizes.

Job analysis should be helpful, but often makes unwarranted assumptions about the personality characteristics for a role, especially if that role is relatively unusual. It is also a problem for newly created roles where there is lack of information about who has been more or less successful within the role. Again, the ideal profile lacks an empirical base in employee selection.

Danger Zone Profiles

On completing the test, I met the consultant for my interview. He was sweating as he looked at me and then at my profile. Glancing down, I could see most of my scores appeared to be in some kind of red danger zone.

I explained I had completed the questionnaire literally and honestly. He was pleasant enough and we had an interesting conversation. He seemed reassured that I was not in fact a sociopath. After the session, the consultant - less sweaty now - asked me why I had been so literal and honest? I did not get the job. **Interviewee on completing a well-known personality assessment**

This approach applies profiles to map thresholds of low and high scale scores indicative of risks within a candidate's personality profile. Danger zone profiles often operate on the Goldilocks principle: too little or too much of any personality trait can be counter-productive. These can either be generated by expert judgement or from a local validation study.

These provide a risk assessment to highlight any potential constraints to the individual's work effectiveness. It is a good strategy. The dominant recruitment philosophy has been to select in for exceptional levels of success. That is often too much of an ask. It is more pragmatic to screen out to avoid damaging failure.[80]

If my job was to pick a group of 10 stocks that would out-perform the average, I wouldn't start by picking the 10 best. I would pick the 10 or 15 worst performers and take them out of the sample, and work with the residual. Start with failure and engineer its removal.
Warren Buffett

Charlie Munger makes the point that exceptional success is extraordinarily difficult to predict. This is the lollapalooza effect requiring the interaction of several extremely positive factors at the right time and a huge slice of luck. It is far simpler to focus on the predictable traits indicative of failure.[81] In practice, danger zones profiles are derived from small sample sizes that fail to replicate in cross validation studies.

Whilst the intuitive approaches should have value, there is little evidence to substantiate these claims. As Yogi Berra observed: i*n theory there is no difference between theory and practice. In practice there is.* In **theory**, the deployment of personality testing as part of the selection interview has intuitive appeal. Disentangling test data from expert judgement to evaluate relative predictive gain has been problematic in **practice**.

It's the actual demonstrated predictive accuracy using real data that calls the shots. **Paul Barrett**[82]

Predictive Algorithms

I*n the era of Big Data we are deluged with false positives*. **Nate Silver**

In the classic article Clinical versus Statistical Prediction[83] Paul Meehl studied the successes and failures of predictions across different settings. He found overwhelming evidence that predictions based on statistical scoring were generally more accurate than those based on expert judgment. This is reminiscent of the specification equations of Ray Cattell's personality questionnaire, the 16PF, of the 1970s Here various traits were combined in a mathematical formula. For example, in the selection of sales people:

Sales success = .44A - .11B - .22E + .11F + .22H......

Future performance is predicted by weighting specific personality factors. Largely a failure at the time, this approach has now been revitalised with the recent wave of the predictive analytics promised by Big Data.

There has been a shift now away from the informal judgement of the assessor to more systematic ways of utilising personality data in selection, particularly in high volume recruitment scenarios. Organisational recruitment practice has moved to the deployment of algorithms that can measure candidate suitability, particularly at the pre-screening phase of the selection process.[84] There are two concerns with the deployment of Big Data predictive analytics in employee selection. One, do they work? Second, are there unintended consequences?

Do these analytics actually work?

Just use computer-based regression and correlation analysis to find statistically significant influences, then combine them to get a perfect fit to the data. When a data set is left to speak for itself like this, it typically spouts nonsense. **Professor Robert Matthews**

The suspicion is that often proprietary algorithms derived from Big Data are based on the art of finding spurious correlations.[85] Here the test publishers make predictive claims that fail to replicate with a different data set. If Big Data is in fact Bad Data, random patterns simply result in highly unstable equations with highly questionable selection outcomes.

The real world is more random than regression analyses. **Nassim Taleb**[86]

Less well understood in the application of analytics is the predictive paradox. When algorithms do improve accuracy and these formulae are used in selection decision making, the model then changes. A cause has a consequence and this consequence shifts the causal dynamic for future prediction.

This paradox resulted in the scenario in which Google, of all firms, made the decision to abandon the use of the cognitive ability tests. Its analytics team found zero correlation between test results and subsequent performance. Google's talent management team had forgotten the problem of restriction of range. If the majority of shortlisted candidates are at the 95th percentile or above on a test, why would we expect much differentiation in performance from the test scores within a very highly selected group? But because Google is viewed by many as an exemplar of best practice, other *follow the leader* companies followed suit and stopped using cognitive testing.

Gerd Gigerenzer[87] makes the point that complex decision algorithms are highly fragile and sensitive to change. A complex formula might improve predictive power for a specific role, but any modest shifts in role requirements will undermine its predictive accuracy.[88] Statistical methods for selection may be robust in low change environments, but wobble badly in the context of change and uncertainty.

T*he bottom line is that if you have lots of data and the world isn't changing too much, you can use statistical methods. For questions with more uncertainty, human experts become more important.* **Lyle Ungar**[89]

It was Paul Meehl himself, in a not well remembered observation, who asked: *Shall we use our heads or shall we follow the formula? Mostly we will use our heads because there just isn't any formula.* Or as Robert Matthews put it: *in the face of uncertainty about the model, the shiny toys of fancy maths have to give way to experience and judgement. With so many reputations resting on regression, it will be a brave researcher who decides to find out how much is baloney.*

Are there any negative unintended consequences associated with predictive analytics?

It's important to remember that big data all comes from the same place - the past. **Rory Sutherland**

Predictive algorithms are not for the faint hearted. There are risks - reputational, legal and financial. When Amazon[90] adopted Artificial Intelligence to review job applicant resumes, the noble intention was to widen the talent pool by scanning the internet for suitable candidates. The consequence: the new recruiting engine did not like women. Amazon's machine learning had been trained to check applicants by observing patterns in resumes submitted over a ten year period. The problem for Amazon: the training set was overwhelmingly based on a male data set, a reflection of male dominance across the tech industry.

Amazon, after several attempts to fix the problem, abandoned the project. Jordan Weissmann[91] notes: *What happened at Amazon really highlights that using such technology without unintended consequences is hard. And if a company like Amazon can't pull it off without problems, it's difficult to imagine that less sophisticated companies can.*

The argument is not that that Big Data and predictive analytics have no place in employee selection. They do. We can anticipate more take-up in screening systems in future selection systems. Instead the recommendation is to avoid the mindless pursuit of correlations in the absence of a defensible theory of context, cause and consequence. And to apply greater diligence in the design and implementation of these statistical approaches, and monitor the longer-term impact.

Neither is it the contention that predictive analytics are inherently discriminatory.[92] Badly implemented however, there is much scope for legal challenge and reputational damage. A cursory review of the web sites of the assessment predictive analytical wonks indicate these firms are ill equipped to address these ethical and legal threats. A prediction - based on intuition not on any algorithm - several vendors are going to take a financial hit as a consequence of the indefensible use of these predictive algorithms in selection.

It's not the crunching power that counts. It's how you use it. **Super Forecaster Philip Tetlock**

In summary, intuition based on expert judgement applied within personality testing in employee selection is low risk, but its value hinges on the wisdom of the assessor. Empirical approaches that deploy statistical methods should be an improvement on intuition. But there is remarkably little evidence in employee selection to indicate this is the case. Algorithms to predict the future based on past patterns drawn from an out-dated dataset will simply replay irrelevance or bias.

It may be the *combination of statistical and judgemental methods is associated with the highest predictive accuracy.*[93]

WHY SO MUCH CAUTION AFTER 70 YEARS

It is strongly recommended that intending users should proceed with due caution. The combination of its psychometric properties, together with the lack of conceptual clarity regarding the nature and significance of the L pattern, raise questions, for both academic researchers and practitioners alike. **British Psychological Society test review of a DISC based instrument**

In the review of the research evidence for personality testing within employee selection, the caution word is repeated with alarming frequency. Caution:

- in the **analysis of research findings** and in the manuals and white papers provided by the test publishers, and the test reviews summarised by professional bodies.
- in the **interpretation of validity evidence** and the extent to which the results from a concurrent design can inform practice within a specific selection scenario.

- over the **usage of response distortion scales**. The tactics to identify and mitigate faking are ineffective and should be jettisoned.
- in how **personality test data should be weighted** and incorporated with a selection decision making process to either screen out or select in candidates.
- in responding to the challenges around **privacy and the legal defensibility** of personality test usage.

If after 100 years of effort in the design, validation and implementation of personality tests, **caution** remains the dominant recommendation, then it may be that the game is up. There are three stances for the future of personality testing in the high stakes scenario of employee selection.

Abandonment of this Enterprise

Maps by their very nature are discarded when a new and better one comes along. Even their name suggests this, which means Latin for napkin. **Ray Talson**

There remains a lack of consensus within the informed community of researchers and practitioners about the predictive validity of self report personality instruments in selection. Debates that go back to the mid-20th century remain unresolved. Despite a massive research programme that has generated several thousand articles over the last few decades, there is no indication that these issues will be resolved.

There are two positions within the abandonment argument. The more **forgiving perspective** is that personality testing adds little value in selection decision making. It incorporates unnecessary organisational time and cost, but is relatively harmless. And profiling may have a useful role to play in personal and team development as part of induction and facilitating key organisational transitions.

The **tougher contention** replays the position of William Whyte and Martin Gross to suggest personality tests are detrimental to the selection of the talent that drives innovation. Faking, for example, appears to be prevalent, and the proposed solutions to mitigate its effects may undermine validity in selection. In many instances, the efforts of the test publishers are the problem not the solution.

Personnel selection advances by discarding those methods that have no predictive value. Graphology was once marketed as a tool in employee selection. Despite the best attempts of a few advocates, it has largely disappeared from the assessment landscape.[94] The experimental and innovative is to be encouraged to explore how to optimise selection processes.

There comes a time however when specific methods have to be thrown aboard. The abandonment perspective suggests that self report personality measures now go into the selection archives of methods that once displayed potential but lacked performance when put to the test.

Incremental Gains Improve Validity

The more interesting question is not whether personality tests show some validity, but rather why they do not do better. **Kevin Murphy**

The more up-beat argument claims that there is sufficient promise from the research base for possible improvements in self report personality test validity. This is the argument of marginal gains which, if implemented by test publishers, will establish personality testing as a valuable tool in selection. This strategy also appeals to practitioners to draw on a broader portfolio of tests for different applications rather than fall back on the assumption that every selection problem is a nail that needs to be hammered with one favoured test.

The proliferation of constructs and measures is not a sign of a healthy science. Rather it shows the inability of empirical studies to demonstrate that a measure is not valid or that a construct may not exist. This is mostly due to self-serving biases and motivated reasoning of test developers.[95]

As part of the marginal gains argument, there is also a greater need to work backwards from the criterion of job performance rather than start with the solution of a personality assessment. This stance also argues for greater methodological rigour to build the evidence base for personality test validity. A shift away from trait theory in thinking about the construction of new personality tests will help.

But personality tests in selection can only become credible as valid instruments when the wider issues facing the psychology profession are addressed.[96] Here there is a move towards the better design of validation studies and an accommodation of the reality of situational specificity rather than the reliance on claims of validity generalisation.

Another key element for practitioners is access to a more informed understanding of how predictive validity is determined and reported. Validity is not the absolute property of a personality test. Any claims by a personality test publisher of 90% predictive accuracy should be a red flag of naiveté or duplicity.

The incremental gains philosophy will also find better ways of integrating personality test data within the sequence of selection decision making.

A Fundamental Rethink

What is new in psychology is not good and what is good is not new.
Professor David Krech in 1949

To paraphrase, what is new in personality testing is not good and what is good is not new.

A rethink is the proposal that personality does shape behaviour and performance in important ways within the work place. But the off-the-shelf self report measures available from the conventional test publishers are ineffective in tapping into this dynamic.

Among the competing products developed by psychologists, perhaps the most important are their assessment instruments.

Unfortunately, in psychology we have no consumers union to test competing claims and to compare these products on their overall effectiveness.

The testing industry provides minor cosmetic successive variants of the same product where only the numbers after the names substantially change.

These variants survive because psychologists buy the tests and then loyally defend them. **Sternberg and Williams**[97]

Despite changes in questionnaire content and response formats, the attempts of quasi-ipsative measures to manage faking, or the deployment of selection decision-making algorithms, conventional self report personality questionnaires have inherent flaws in employee selection to limit predictive power.

What are the options for practitioners? Are there promising future directions?

FUTURE DIRECTIONS

The Shift Towards Contextualised Applications

There was a time when the deployment of generic instruments was the only cost effective option. These personality tests it was claimed provided tried and tested solutions with known psychometric properties, access to an extensive normative database and established predictive validity. This claim is misplaced. There is reason to think that a move towards more bespoke design targeted at specific occupational groupings and roles represents a more promising way forward. Contextualisation helps. *Adding context doubled the validity of personality measures.*[98]

Asked what recommendations would you give about the use of personality tests in selection contexts, Neal Schmitt's response: *First avoid published personality measures in most instances. Second, I would construct my own measures that are linked directly to job tasks in a face-valid or relevant fashion.*

There is still some debate over whether broad or narrow constructs provide greater predictive power. On the one hand, *narrow traits seem to add incremental validity to the Big 5 in correlations with managerial success.*[99] On the other hand, there is a question mark about narrow measures. Many of the traits measured by personality scales may simply not exist.

Very very exciting news. A new personality trait has been discovered. The need for Drama.[100]

Scales based on items that are near synonyms has become a common publisher tactic for impressive - but spurious - reliability estimates. This is the bloated specific called out by Ray Cattell several decades ago. These tests simply show that candidates understand the meaning of words and are prepared to tolerate test publisher repetition. There is little evidence that this strategy made any predictive gains.

A variation of this approach is the jingle jangle factor. When we assume two different applications are the same because they have the same label, this is jingle. When we think two similar applications are different because they have different labels, this is jangle.[101]

The world of psychological tests jangles more noisily than a gamelan orchestra. **Professor Adrian Furnham**

A new test is announced with snap, crackle and pop. When, for example, Grit appeared on the scene, the marketing claimed:

self-discipline accounts for more than twice as much variance as IQ. Grit sounded different and practitioners assumed it was different. As it turned out, Grit was largely a combination of Big 5 personality traits and added little to prediction. It may even have had negative consequences.[102]

Bespoke development has become a more realistic testing strategy given innovations in open access item banks, agile project management and a new generation of on line technology tools. In addition, the practitioner market is showing signs of impatience with the take it or leave it philosophy of the conventional test publishers. Publisher demands for expensive training and further accreditation face challenge.

Extending the concept of customisation, we can anticipate not only more bespoke measures at an organisational level, but greater personalisation for the individual candidate in completion. Adaptive testing is now common practice in the domain of aptitudes. More recently, there have been advances to apply this approach in personality testing.

This shifts profiling to an idiographic philosophy rather than continue to rely on the conventional (but now highly suspect) nomothetic design.[103] Probably impractical for high volume recruitment, the personalised test strategy has much virtue in assessments that require a detailed understanding of the individual in their own unique context.

The fundamental shift in the market place is now towards contextualised and customised applications to move away from generic measures that claim to work in any selection scenario.

Tailor made, context specific measures may yield superior validity to the Big 5 measures. **Neal Schmitt**

Objective Metrics

As I grow older, I pay less attention to what people say. I simply watch what they do. **Andrew Carnegie**

In Everybody Lies, Seth Stephens-Davidowitz[104] builds on the thesis of Peter Thiel who noted that Facebook and Netflix have built their businesses on the principle: *Don't trust people on what they say. Trust what they do.* Asking individuals, for example, about their sexual preferences reveals one story. Accessing their browser search history provides a different account. Or, as the Netflix data scientist Xavier Amatrian notes: *The algorithms know you better than you know yourself.* No doubt much exaggerated hype in this claim.

This is reminiscent of biodata, a methodology that goes back several decades with decent predictive validity. Biodata measures are constructed around previous life experience and achievements. Above all, candidate responses are verifiable, at least in principle.

The single item: have you ever built a model plane that flew out-performed an entire battery of aptitude tests in the prediction of US navy pilot training success.

This approach indicates that subjective self report measures need to be replaced by more objective metrics of personality. There are any number of facts that we can access about an individual's personality. Snoop[105] proposes we can obtain important insights *by* looking at stuff: s*tuff in offices, bedrooms, cars and bathrooms. What's there and how it's arranged can provide clues about who we are and what's important to us.*

There are other clues that can be gleaned during these face to face meetings. For example, if, during his interview, he took a second biscuit with his cup of tea, this might provide a clue for the self-indulgence measure, which looks at how easily tempted a person is. **David Cooper**

Ludicrous, and not advisable in employee selection. But the concept has some merit provided we avoid stereotypes. We can also review candidate suitability by snooping on social media. Again not without its risks.

Alternatively, we can apply the kind of linguistic analysis in personality profiling as pioneered by IBM's Watson.[106] Here Watson analyses text data from emails, blogs, tweets and other social media to generate a candidate personality profile. At this stage, this is an enterprise based more on trust rather than evidence.

Hiring a private detective to shadow a candidate would also gather public information that might be relevant, yet most people would view it as an unacceptable invasion of privacy.

Peter Cappelli[107]

HireVue in its selection systems deployed proprietary algorithms to analyse facial movements, word choice and speaking in candidate webcam interviews to generate an employability score. But it is difficult to evaluate the predictive accuracy of this approach. *500,000 data points to provide superhuman precision and impartiality to zero in on the ideal personality* seems impressive. But as Carl Sagan reminded us: *Extraordinary claims require extraordinary evidence.* The extraordinary evidence is unavailable.[108] Here the black box of the predictive formulae is inaccessible for any meaningful evaluation of validity or fairness.

Whatever the level of predictive accuracy is claimed or found, this methodology is not without its critics. Meredith Whittaker at the AI Institute suggests: *It's pseudo-science. And a licence to discriminate.*

And it is clear there are genuine ethical difficulties with a tool that doesn't explain its decisions or give candidates their assessment scores. Given the status of the evidence base and concerns that unsuccessful candidates will challenge selection decisions, this approach to personality testing requires a robust risk assessment. But the principle is sound. Objective and verifiable metrics[109] should out-perform subjective self report measures. The challenge is ensuring that the shift towards the capture and utilisation of these kinds of metrics in employee selection is defensible. Defensible as genuine predictors of future performance, and defensible in complying with data protection and privacy legislation.

The Rediscovery of Projective Tests

There is a powerful force within us, an un-illuminated part of the mind – separate from the conscious mind that is constantly at work moulding our thought, feelings, and actions. **Sigmund Freud**

Rorschach ink blots, the Thematic Apperception Test, the Sentence Completion Test and the like have gone into the archives of selection stuff that might work but failed to cut the validity mustard. Nathan Carter[110] outlines a convincing case why we should revisit the concept of projective testing. Experiments to translate these kinds of projective measures from clinical applications to organisational contexts in the 1960s had mixed results. Carter argues there is sufficient promise to suggest that practitioners should continue to explore projective methodologies.

Arguably most projective measures were developed from out-dated psychological theory, often psycho-analytical. A move towards more contemporary perspectives on personality that avoids any intrusive assessment represents a more promising direction. Along these lines, the Cambridge Code's personality test - an X Ray of the Subconscious Mind - includes the question: *"Have you ever had an imaginary twin?"* An interesting line of direction, but the claim of: *"proven to uncover the subconscious latent potential"* seems premature.[111]

The rediscovery of projective tests also reflects the trend towards more image based approaches in personality testing.[112] This new wave of methodologies may well improve candidate engagement, reduce user fatigue and shorten completion times. Visually based assessments may also have the potential to be more accessible to those with language or learning difficulties or for candidates from different cultural backgrounds.

A similar design philosophy is also used in the application of gamification[113], now increasingly deployed in assessments of cognitive aptitude and personality. No doubt there is much vendor hype about new developments in image based tests. But greater innovation in personality assessment through advances in, for example, Virtual Reality[114] seems likely.

Traditional tests seem increasingly out of touch. Why? Because the user experience is often incredibly poor. Many tests still involve almost always endless word-crunching. The bigger problem is that they don't tap into what we humans are best at: visual processing.
Heather Myers

It may be that DNA testing is the future for personality assessment in employee selection. For any number of reasons, this is doubtful at least in the medium term. We need to look for innovation elsewhere.

CONCLUSIONS

While predictive models and data-driven approaches can improve hiring decisions, human judgment, intuition, and adaptability are also crucial. **ChatGTP4**

In Pitfalls of Personality Theory, Colin Cooper indicates that complacency is rarely the route to progress.[115] The personality testing industry has been lazy. In a replay of the mid-20th century, today's publishers have relied too much on the recycling of previous generations of self report measures.

And unto the Woodworth Personal Data Sheet was born the Bernreuter Personality Inventory. In those days there many sons and daughters, Guilford-Zimmerman Temperament Survey and Thurstone Personality Schedule. And also the 16P. And the 16PF begat the OPQ and also the 15FQ. And the OPQ begat WAVE and TalentQ Dimensions. And these begat many more.

Me Too imitation has done little to advance either theory or practice in personality assessment for employee selection. This strategy of keeping up with the Joneses has failed. The gap between the hype of marketing claim and the evidence of predictive validity has widened. It is unlikely that future variations - in our understanding of personality and how it shapes performance outcomes, or through the deployment of new technology - will transform the predictive power of personality measurement in employee selection. A shift in theory, design philosophy and decision making principles will be required.

Personality - unlike intelligence - is an especially unruly selection method. Modest improvement seems to be a more realistic goal. But **validity** is not the only issue in how we apply personality measures in selection.

The **engagement of candidates** in the recruitment process is also critical. What does the choice of personality assessments indicate about the organisation? Quick, fast paced and interesting tests in employee selection send out one cultural message. Time-consuming, repetitive and dull tests used by pretty much every other company project a different message about the firm's culture. How does our personality testing strategy engage the candidates we want to attract?

The other key consideration in the choice of assessment methodology is the agenda for **greater inclusion and diversity**. Much of the rationale behind the use of personality tests in employee selection was the claim of a reduction in adverse impact vis a vis for example cognitive tests.[116] This argument is now challenged.

Companies that emphasize neuroscience, big data, and gamification may be trying to distract you from the fact that their assessments don't predict workplace performance. **Ryne Sherman**[117]

The use of current self report personality tests from the main stream test publishers in the high stakes scenario of employee selection is now highly questionable. Until we shift to:

- **contextualised and customised measures**.
- the addition of **objective metrics** rather than rely only on subjective self report measures.
- the greater use of image-based assessments for a more **engaging candidate experience** that avoid repetitive tedium.
- personality assessments that are **genuinely inclusive**; tests that aren't designed and validated only with WEIRD samples - Western, Educated, Industrialised, Rich, and Democratic.[118]

we can only anticipate another century of counter-productive debate and confusing claims in which self report personality test data from applicants account for at best less than 5% of work performance. At worst, the continued usage of conventional personality testing in selection will undermine business productivity and innovation.

NOTES

1. From the vendor site: "45000+ The number of statements in our database, from which we create each tailored report. The high accuracy of our reports is due to the excellent performance of our questionnaire algorithm and the bank of statements we draw from.

   This is a meaningless statement, and the site fails to provide any evidence of gains in employee engagement, team effectiveness or business impact. No doubt the vendor would express horror at the way its tool is being used. But when a personality assessment is sold like office stationery to Uncle Tom Cobley and all, these are the adverse consequences.

   In the documentary Persona: The Dark Truth Behind Personality Tests, the discriminatory nature of a widely used tool is put under the microscope; https://www.theguardian.com/tv-and-radio/2021/mar/03/they-become-dangerous-tools-the-dark-side-of-personality-tests

2. Which personality test is best was once a much loved topic of LinkedIn discussion groups, an exercise in which the vendors made extravagant claims of their specific tests. This is not new. The world of personality testing has been characterised by debate about the best test. This seems the wrong way to think

about personality testing. Different tests seem to work better for different purposes. The practitioner search for the "best test" may be a factor in explaining why gains in predictive validity in selection have been limited.

A Review and Comparison of 12 personality Inventories on Key Psychometrics, Prewett et al; Handbook of Personality at Work

The Comparative Validity of 11 Modern Personality Inventories: Predictions of Behavioral Acts, Informant Reports, and Clinical Indicators; https://projects.ori.org/lrg/PDFs_papers/Grucza&Goldberg_2007_JPA.pdf

3. Controversies. Controversy has been a running theme in personality testing over the years. The episode of Cambridge Analytica's personality test and the harvesting of personal data was another in a long line of challenges about how test data is captured and used. https://slate.com/technology/2018/04/how-corporations-convinced-us-that-personality-tests-are-fun.html

4. Disgraced former Co-op Bank chairman Paul Flowers did very well in psychometric tests in interviews for the role, a committee of MPs has heard. Mr Flowers, a Methodist minister with little experience in banking, became chairman of the Coop board in April 2010, with a disastrous outcome. A rescue deal was

required with bondholders after it emerged the bank faced a £1.5bn black hole.

https://www.theguardian.com/business/blog/2014/jan/31/paul-flowers-psychometric-testing-bank-chairman

5. This mirrors a more general problem within the psychological sciences. The ability of scientific psychology to explain variance has not improved in 60 years of ever increasing research activity. Smedslund, G., Arnulf, J.K., & Smedslund, J. (2022). Is psychological science progressing? Frontiers in Psychology: Theoretical and Philosophical Psychology, 13

https://www.frontiersin.org/articles/10.3389/fpsyg.2022.1089089

6. The One Million Dollar Paranormal Challenge;

https://www.thevintagenews.com/2016/12/30/james-randi-created-the-one-million-dollar-paranormal-challenge-no-one-ever-claimed-the-prize/

7. Research design. This kind of longitudinal research requires a combination of methodological savvy and a commitment to the long-term. But this is not new. Over 70 years ago, William Whyte outlined the required design: a rigorous validation requires that a firm tests applicants on the new personality test, seals away the results so that the test scores don't influence either the selection decision or bias managers in their view of the successful recruits. And then matches the test data against performance at a later time.

8. The Validity of Personality Inventories in the Selection of Employees, Ghiselli & Barthol, 1953; Validity Of Personality Measures In Personnel Selection; Robert M. Guion Richard F. Gottier, 1965

9. Robert Gibby & Michael Zickar, A history of the early days of testing in American industry: an obsession with adjustment, History of Psychology, September 2008 https://www.researchgate.net/publication/23562101_A_history_of_the_early_days_of_personality_testing_in_American_industry_An_obsession_with_adjustment

10. The Tyranny of Personality Testing; https://newrepublic.com/article/151098/personality-brokers-book-review-invention-myers-briggs-type-indicator More on the Myers Briggs Type Indicator. A head to head contest with astrology; http://matteroffactsblog.wordpress.com/2013/11/21/is-myers-briggs-any-better-than-a-horoscope/

11. Are norm groups sexist: https://qz.com/1201773/we-took-the-worlds-most-scientific-personality-test-and-discovered-unexpectedly-sexist-results/ Norm groups are problematic in personality testing. "Because if the norm group characteristics change in any way, the entire benchmarking process is rendered problematic. More importantly, if score magnitudes are considered related to performance, then it is the actual score which carries that

relationship, not its "normed-percentile", sten, or T-score version." Normative Test Scores in a Performance-Oriented Personnel Selection Strategy, Paul Barrett; https://www.pbarrett.net/stratpapers/normscore.pdf

Add to the problem, scale skew, low reliability and norms assembled from convenience samples rather than applicant groups, and the candidate intention in questionnaire completion is distorted in the report outputs.

12. An odd quote. It was during a time when IBM adopted a highly prescribed dress code including appropriate sock length.

13. For an incisive analysis of the challenges and constraints of Big Data, Chancing It: The Laws of Chance and How They Can Work for You, Robert Matthews

14. Validity, Reliability, and Baloney; https://journals.sagepub.com/doi/10.1177/001316445001000107

15. For example, Barrick, M. R. and Mount, M. K. (1991). The Big Five personality dimensions and job performance: A meta-analysis. Personnel Psychology 44(1): https://doi.org/10.1111/j.1744-6570.1991.tb00688.x

16. Why Personality Measures Have Limited Applicability in Personnel Selection, Kevin R. Murphy Jessica L. Dzieweczynski

Morgeson, F., Campion, M., Dipboye, R., Hollenbeck, J., Murphy, K., Schmitt, N. (2007b). Are we getting fooled again? Coming to terms with limitations in the use of personality tests for personnel selection. Personnel Psychology, 60, 1029-1049

17. The Power of Personality The Comparative Validity of Personality Traits, Socioeconomic Status, and Cognitive Ability for Predicting Important Life Outcomes; https://www.ncbi.nlm.nih.gov/pmc/articles/PMC4499872

    Robust Findings in Personality Psychology https://pigee.wordpress.com/2019/11/12/robust-findings-in-personality-psychology/

18. The Forer effect; http://forer.netopti.net/
    Dickson D & Kelly I (1985) The Barnum effect in personality assessment, Psychological Reports, 57
    Also: Stephen J. Guastello, Denise D. Guastello & Larry L. Craft (1989) Assessment of the Barnum Effect in Computer-Based Test Interpretations, The Journal of Psychology

19. Publication Bias in Test Publishers' Manual. A Case Study of Four Test Vendors, Michael McDaniel; https://citeseerx.ist.psu.edu/document?repid=rep1&type=pdf&doi=eb2ba7d45bae0bf84a8679ffc500be6a4a4d03c4

20. The halo effect, and other managerial delusions, Phil Rosenzweig; https://en.wikipedia.org/wiki/The_Halo_Effect_(business_book)

21. The results from 360° feedback applications create further problems in personality test validation. When line management ratings are only modestly correlated with those from peers, team members and other stakeholders, which group has the most informed and accurate view of effectiveness? In most datasets, peer-team member correlations are highest and correlations between management perceptions and team member views are extremely low.

Which validity coefficients should be applied when there is a such a divergence of evaluations of effectiveness?

22. This claim was reported:
http://www.psychometricsdirect.co.uk/psychometrics/comparing-the-opq-with-the-saville-consulting-wave-personality-assessments
From the Emergenetics web site, now withdrawn.

23. The Validity and Utility of Selection Methods in Personnel Psychology: Practical and Theoretical Implications of 100 Years" Frank Schmidt;
https://www.researchgate.net/publication/309203898_The_Validity_and_Utility_of_Selection_Methods_in_Personnel_Psychology_Practical_and_Theoretical_Implications_of_100_Years_of_Research_Findings

24. For more on the debate on validity generalisation vis a vis situational specificity, What Personality Does and Does Not

Predict and Why: Lessons Learned and Future Directions;
https://www.academia.edu/33781689/What_Personality_Does_a
nd_Does_Not_Predict_and_Why_Lessons_Learned_and_Future_Di
rections?email_work_card=view-paper

25. Even Conscientiousness, viewed as the most conscientious of all
the Big Five traits to generalise, looks problematic. The validity
of conscientiousness is moderately overestimated (by around
30%).
http://www.people.vcu.edu/~mamcdani/Publications/Kepes%20
&%20McDaniel%20(2015).%20Validity%20of%20conscientiousne
ss%20PLoS%20One.pdf

26. Sackett. P.R., Zhang, C., Berry, C.M., & Lievens, F. (2023).
Revisiting the design of selection systems in light of new
findings regarding the validity of widely used predictors.
Industrial and Organizational Psychology: Perspectives on
Science and Practice, awaiting commentaries, pp.1-37.
https://lnkd.in/gnEyecYE

    Paul Barrett summarises the results of four meta-analytical
    studies;
    https://www.linkedin.com/feed/update/urn:li:activity:703084802
    5090547713/

27. Who is your expert;
https://www.youtube.com/watch?v=lADB9Qu53CY

28. Scatter plots and what does a correlation of .5 look like? https://janhove.github.io/teaching/2016/11/21/what-correlations-look-like

29. On natural frequencies; https://understandinguncertainty.org/using-expected-frequencies-when-teaching-probability

30. Flawed Self-Assessment: Implications for Health, Education, and the Workplace; https://www.ncbi.nlm.nih.gov/pubmed/26158995

    Zell, E., & Krizan, Z. (2014). Do people have insight into their abilities? A metasynthesis. Perspectives on Psychological Science, 9(2) http://dx.doi.org/10.1177/1745691613518075

31. Deceit and Self-Deception, Robert Trivers. A review; https://www.theguardian.com/science/2011/oct/07/deceit-self-deception-robert-trivers

    Surprising results that counter the popular idea that knowing yourself is good for you; https://www.scientificamerican.com/article/new-insights-into-self-insight-more-may-not-be-better/

32. On the Dunning-Kruger Effect; https://theness.com/neurologicablog/index.php/lessons-from-dunning-kruger/

As it turns out this is not straightforward. What the Dunning-Kruger effect is and isn't;
https://www.talyarkoni.org/blog/2010/07/07/what-the-dunning-kruger-effect-is-and-isnt/

33. CEO Overconfidence and Corporate Investment; Malmendier & Tate
https://onlinelibrary.wiley.com/doi/full/10.1111/j.1540-6261.2005.00813.x

34. Some people are irritable, but everyone likes to visit museums: what personality inventories tell us about how we're all just like one another;
https://www.talyarkoni.org/blog/tag/psychometrics/

35. Griffith & Converse, 2011;
https://www.oxfordscholarship.com/view/10.1093/acprof:oso/9780195387476.001.0001/acprof-9780195387476-chapter-003

36. Ones, D.S. and Viswesvaran, C. (1997), A meta-analytic investigation of social desirability influences on integrity test validities: much ado about nothing

37. A Socioanalytic View of Faking;
https://www.advancedpeoplestrategies.co.uk/media/1134/a-socioanalytic-view-of-faking.pdf

In Why the Fake You will Outperform the Authentic You, there is no evidence for the claim that I fake, and you should do,

because it is scientifically proven to make you a higher performer.
https://www.talentstrategygroup.com/application/third_party/c
kfinder/userfiles/files/Why%20the%20Fake%20You%20will%20O
utperform.pdf

38. We are back to the William Whyte position that sees personality testing in selection as a kind of filter to check conservative conformity rather than identify distinctive personality. This is to value candidate gamesmanship rather than sincerity.

39. The Gervais Principle, Or The Office According to The Office;
https://www.ribbonfarm.com/2009/10/07/the-gervais-principle-
or-the-office-according-to-the-office/
Book et al found enabled faking good respondents had higher psychopathy scores than individuals caught faking.
Bonnie M. MacNeil, Ronald R. Holden, 2006, Psychopathy and the detection of faking on self-report inventories of personality

40. https://www.predictiveindex.com/blog/how-to-pass-a-
personality-test-and-common-questions-on-faking-
assessments/

41. Are the consequences of these claimed levels of failure a result of the increased usage of personality testing?
https://www.hoganassessments.com/bad-management-and-
its-consequences/

42. Remarkably, the advocates of faking is good point out that the base rate of failure for managers in is about 65%" https://www.hoganassessments.com/blog/abstracting-leadership/ At this rate of failure, it is astonishing that economic activity continues.

Professor Adrian Furnham at UCL, associated with Thomas International as well as Hogan Assessments, provides a slide on the abysmal rates of management failure. Drilling into his 40 - 50% estimate, very different definitions, criteria, samples and methodologies are applied. Bentz was a small scale study of failed managers in retail, followed up by a McCall Lombardo study based on 20 senior executives in 3 companies. Milliken-Davies' estimate, an unpublished dissertation, drew on data from first line supervisors in a large aerospace company. Shipper & Wilson's figure of 60% is derived from a US hospital. How any patient survived that hospital is extraordinary. DeVries suggests the failure rate among senior executives in corporate America has been at least 50% which is odd given that only 2% of CEOs are fired for under-performance. It's not clear how Charan obtained his figure.

In summary, an exaggerated methodological mess. No decent study for this Chicken Little claim of management disaster gives a convincing rationale for these estimates.

43. A 55% drop in validity for Conscientiousness and a 67% for Agreeableness; Griffith, R. L., & Converse, P. D. (2012). The rules

of evidence and the prevalence of applicant faking. In M. Ziegler, C. MacCann, & R. D. Roberts (Eds.), New perspectives on faking in personality assessment

44. Christiansen, N. D., Rozek, R. F., & Burns, G. (2010). Effects of social desirability scores on hiring judgments. Journal of Personnel Psychology, 9(1), 27-39. http://dx.doi.org/10.1027/1866-5888/a000003

    Faking and selection: Considering the use of personality from select-in and select-out perspectives, The Journal of applied psychology; https://www.researchgate.net/publication/10773192_Faking_and_selection_Considering_the_use_of_personality_from_select-in_and_select-out_perspectives

45. Bizarrely, the site goes on to provide: 4 Key tips to pass the SHL OPQ; https://www.graduatesfirst.com/employer-tests/shl-occupational-personality-questionnaire-opq

46. DISC Based Personality Assessment: the history, current status, and the fascinating life of William Marston; https://talentworldconsulting.com/project/disc-based-personality-assessment

47. Using Overt and Covert Items in Self-Report Personality Tests: Susceptibility to Faking and Identifiability of Possible Fakers; https://www.ncbi.nlm.nih.gov/pmc/articles/PMC6037895/

48. It is easier to design and sell a personality test with obvious transparency than one which requires any deep insight into the complexities of psychology and personality.

49. It was Cyril Burt, albeit disgraced after his own faking antics in research into identical twins, who made the point: when an applicant completes an intelligence test they are also completing a personality test. And when completing a personality test, also an intelligence test. Social Desirability Response scales require skills in verbal critical reasoning.

50. The Red Herring Needs to be Grilled: Issues of Social Desirability in Personality Testing, Rosanna Miguel;
https://www.academia.edu/22338855/The_Red_Herring_Needs_to_be_Grilled_Issues_of_Social_Desirability_in_Personality_Testing

    Kiefer, C. and Benit, N. (2016). What is Applicant Faking Behavior? A Review on the Current State of Theory and Modelling Techniques. Journal of European journal of European Psychology Students

    Schmitt & Oswald, The Impact of Corrections for Faking on the Validity of Noncognitive Measures in Selection
https://www.researchgate.net/publication/7046252_The_Impact_of_Corrections_for_Faking_on_the_Validity_of_Noncognitive_Measures_in_Selection_Settings

51. Another perspective on retesting. With so much riding on the outcome of job screening personality tests, it's probably not

surprising that failing candidates who opted to take retake the test would deliberately change their responses. https://digitalcommons.ilr.cornell.edu/cgi/viewcontent.cgi?article=1019&context=cahrs_researchlink

Sackett PR, Burris LR, Ryan AM (1989). Coaching and practice effects in personnel selection. International review of industrial and organizational psychology

52. Faking in Personality Assessment, Carolyn Maccann, Matthias Ziegle & Richard Roberts

53. Yes or no? Are Likert scales always preferable to dichotomous rating scales? https://pigee.wordpress.com/2015/11/06/yes-or-no-are-likert-scales-always-preferable-to-dichotomous-rating-scales/

54. This is the Annie Hall factor. In the movie, starring Woody Allen as Alvy Singer and Diane Keaton as Annie Hall, each visit their own psychiatrist to discuss their relationship. https://www.youtube.com/watch?v=O7nPkpdFAic

55. This is illogical. Forced choice design identifies relative preferences for an individual. It does not allow a comparison between individuals. Forced choice outcomes highlight choices - which drink is selected at say a social event. It does not provide the basis for judgements about the extent of alcohol consumption.

Ipsative measurement has its place, specifically in identifying personal priorities within some domains of individual difference in vocational preferences, leadership styles to highlight relative preferences but remain problematic in comparisons across candidates.

The issue of ipsative design for personality measures in employee selection was the focus of a spat within the assessment industry in the late 1980s with the publication of Spurious and spuriouser: the use of ipsative personality tests, Blinkhorn S et al (1988) Journal of Occupational Psychology, 61

The "ipsative debate" continues to the present. Additional commentaries:
The Insignificance of Personality Testing, Steve Blinkhorn and Charles Johnson, Nature, December 1990
https://www.pbarrett.net/publications/Ipsative_Testing_Hammo nd%20_and_Barrett_1996.pdf.
https://oprablog.wordpress.com/2010/10/27/ipsative-tests-psychometric-properties/
https://www.prevuehr.com/resources/insights/ipsative-vs-normative/

The psychometrician Steve Blinkhorn reviews recent attempts to recalibrate ipsative data, for example
https://kar.kent.ac.uk/44775/1/Personality%20assessment%2C %20Forced-choice%20FINAL%20for%20sharing.pdf and makes

the point: "ipsative chalk cannot be turned into normative cheese."

56. Neil D. Christiansen, Gary N. Burns & George E. Montgomery (2005) Reconsidering Forced-Choice Item Formats for Applicant Personality Assessment, Human Performance

Forced-choice assessments of personality for selection: evaluating issues of normative assessment and faking resistance. J Appl Psychol. 2006 Jan;91(1):9-24

Fisher, Peter A.; Robie, Chet; Christiansen, Neil D.; Speer, Andrew B.; and Schneider, Leann (2019) Criterion-related Validity of Forced-Choice Personality Measures: A Cautionary Note Regarding Thurstonian IRT versus Classical Test Theory Scoring, Personnel Assessment and Decisions

Effects of Applicant Faking on Forced-Choice and Likert Scores; Goran Pavlov, Alberto Maydeu-Olivares, Amanda J. Fairchild; http://journals.sagepub.com/doi/pdf/10.1177/1094428117753683

John R. Braun (2018) Forced-Choice Self-Report Devices: A Look at Some Unwarranted Claims, Measurement and Evaluation in Guidance, 2:3

Cao, M., & Western, Educated, Industrialized, Rich, And Democratic, F. (2019, May 9). Does Forcing Reduce Faking? A Meta-Analytic Review of Forced-Choice Personality Measures in High-Stakes Situations. Journal of Applied Psychology. Advance online publication. http://dx.doi.org/10.1037/apl0000414

57. The "g" in Faking: Doublethink the Validity of Personality Self-Report Measures for Applicant Selection https://www.frontiersin.org/articles/10.3389/fpsyg.2018.02153/full

58. There's more to personality than a test score; https://theconversation.com/theres-more-to-personality-than-a-test-score-30898

59. Ironically it was Walter Mischel, one of the most vocal critics of personality traits, who in the marshmallow test observed the importance of delayed gratification as a predictor of life outcomes. His finding was over-turned by additional research which suggested social and economic background, not the ability to delay gratification, lay behind the children's' long-term success.

   New Study Disavows Marshmallow Test's Predictive Powers; https://anderson-review.ucla.edu/new-study-disavows-marshmallow-tests-predictive-powers/

60. Ian Deary also explores the issue of whether traits are simply descriptive or have explanatory value. The Trait Approach to Personality, The Cambridge Handbook of Personality Psychology

61. World's top personality test doesn't really work – should we ditch it? https://www.newscientist.com/article/2209360-worlds-top-personality-test-doesnt-really-work-should-we-ditch-it/

62. Challenges to capture the big five personality traits in non-WEIRD populations;
https://advances.sciencemag.org/content/5/7/eaaw5226
Beck, E. D., Condon, D. M., & Jackson, J. J. (2019, July 9).
Interindividual Age Differences in Personality Structure.
https://doi.org/10.31234/osf.io/857ev

63. Hexaco; http://hexaco.org/scaledescriptions
An alternative framework; Open to experience - closed to intelligence: Why the Big Five are really the Comprehensive Six,
Chris Brand;
https://onlinelibrary.wiley.com/doi/abs/10.1002/per.2410080407

64. The General Factor of Personality: A meta-analysis of Big Five intercorrelations;
https://advances.sciencemag.org/content/5/7/eaaw5226

65. Dan McAdams and three levels of personality;
https://www.psychologytoday.com/gb/blog/the-personality-analyst/201011/three-levels-knowing-person

66. Perspectives on Models of Job Performance;
https://www.researchgate.net/publication/229645528_Perspectives_on_Models_of_Job_Performance

67. A Random Search for Excellence. Why great company research delivers fables and not facts;
https://www2.deloitte.com/us/en/insights/topics/operations/a-

random-search-for-excellence-why-great-company-research-delivers-fables-not-facts.html

68. An empirical investigation of the antecedents, behaviours, and outcomes of bad leadership, Journal of Leadership Studies, 2007; https://onlinelibrary.wiley.com/doi/abs/10.1002/jls.20023

69. Dark side leadership. Harms, P.D., Spain, S., & Hannah, S. (2011). Leader development and the dark side of personality. The Leadership Quarterly, 22

70. The test review process of the British Psychological Society was instrumental in undermining credibility in personality testing in employee selection by lowering standards of predictive validity. The EFPA Test-Review Model: When Good Intentions Meet a Methodological Thought Disorder, Paul Barrett; https://www.ncbi.nlm.nih.gov/pmc/articles/PMC5791023/

71. We revisit the analysis of William Whyte and Martin Gross from the 1960s. Any predictive gain - however questionable - was achieved only by the personality traits of corporate conformity. And conscientiousness has often been the flag waving display of personality testing's achievements. Compliance to regular routines may be a key trait for many roles, but not for those requiring independent thinking for creativity.

72. Jack Welch was named Manager of the 20th century by Fortune magazine. As it turned out the House That Jack Built collapsed very quickly;

https://www.forbes.com/sites/brycehoffman/2015/04/11/ge-tears-down-the-house-that-jack-built/?

73. Witt, L. The Interactive Effects of Extraversion and Conscientiousness on Performance, Journal of Vocational Behavior

74. The influence of work on personality trait development: The demands-affordances transactional (DATA) model, an integrative review, and research agenda, Journal of Vocational Behavior, February 2019

75. In Personality testing in personnel selection: Love it? Leave it? Understand it, Diekman & Konig: Especially in case of tests from commercial publishers, it is often difficult to evaluate how these interpretations are generated, which statistical methods and which interpretative algorithms are used to combine test results.

76. The holistic approach to judgment and prediction has not held up to scientific scrutiny; Highhouse, S. (2002), 'Assessing the Candidate as a Whole: A Historical and Critical Analysis of Individual Psychological Assessment for Personnel Decision Making,' Personnel Psychology
Holistic Assessment for Selection and Placement, Scott Highhouse and John A. Kostek;
https://www.researchgate.net/publication/329322512_Holistic_Assessment_for_Selection_and_Placement

77. More troubling for this strategy, the psychometric position that the interview as an assessment methodology lacks validity has been over turned. The interview - structured and unstructured - stands up better than personality tests in the validity league tables.

    Rethinking The Validity Of Interviews For Employment Decision Making; Oh, I.-S., Postlethwaite, B. E., & Schmidt, F. L. (2013). Rethinking the validity of interviews for employment decision making: Implications of recent developments in meta-analysis There is no evidence that incremental gains in selection interview validity have been achieved through the introduction of personality tests.

78. This mirrors the way in which organisations build brands through expensive advertising. Costly signalling in advertising; https://www.warc.com/newsandopinion/opinion/how-costly-signaling-makes-ads-more-effective/2234

79. The validity period of assessment data; Best practices; https://www.tts-talent.com/blog/he-validity-period-of-assessment-data-best-practices/

80. The Lollapalooza Effect: Berkshire Hathaway, assessment and rethinking talent management; https://talentworldconsulting.com/wp-content/uploads/2023/08/The-Lollapalooza-Effect-Charlie-Munger-Talent-Assessment.pdf

81. There are some roles where more is more. Sales is a good example. Every successful appointment you make has a direct impact on the company's bottom line. So we therefore want to select the outstanding performers. There are some roles however, where less is more. Take the head of safety at a nuclear processing company. Brilliance isn't going to put much on the bottom line, but incompetence will have devastating consequences.
   What does validity mean in assessments and how do we evaluate it?; https://www.evolveassess.com/psyched-for-business/psyched-for-business-podcast-episode-15

82. Paul Barrett and his commentary in Assessments: can't live with 'em, can't live without 'em; http://www.ere.net/2010/03/31/assessments-can%E2%80%99t-live-with-em-can%E2%80%99t-live-without-em/

83. Clinical versus statistical prediction: A theoretical analysis and a review of the evidence; https://psycnet.apa.org/record/2006-21565-000

84. Can Big Data be too clever by half? The irony in which Big Data profiler Nigel Oakes of Strategic Communication Laboratories which spun into Cambridge Analytica was skewered by a simple check of his CV.
   https://www.theguardian.com/politics/2017/mar/04/nigel-oakescambridge-analytica-what-role-brexit-trump

85. Correlations are like coincidences. We'd take them less seriously if we were more aware of how easily we find them. Per capita cheese consumption correlates with the number of people who died by becoming tangled in their bedsheets (r = 0.947).
More spurious correlations;
https://www.tylervigen.com/spurious-correlations
The number of decimal places in a reported correlation coefficient is another red flag of a spurious correlation. The law of phony precision - more than two points - has caught out a few fake findings. Recently, Barbara Fredrickson - "if your ratio was greater than 2.9013 positive emotions to 1 negative emotion you were flourishing in life" - was embarrassed to discover that this exactitude was based on pseudo-science. She acknowledged: "I didn't understand the maths." No one else did either.
The British amateur who debunked the mathematics of happiness;
https://www.theguardian.com/science/2014/jan/19/mathematics-of-happiness-debunked-nick-brown

86. The problem is beyond psychology: The real world is more random than regression analyses;
http://fooledbyrandomness.com/Taleb-Goldstein-IJF2012.pdf

87. Gerd Gigerenzer on heuristics;
https://www.annualreviews.org/doi/abs/10.1146/annurev-psych-120709-145346

Heuristics are often conceived of as a source of systematic error, whereas logic and statistics are regarded as the sine qua non of good decision making. Yet, this view can be incorrect for decisions made under uncertainty, as opposed to risk. Research on fast and frugal heuristics shows that simple heuristics can be successful in complex, uncertain environments and also when and why this is the case.
https://pdfs.semanticscholar.org/06b4/c251a2a27abf732ce2730068161f00300c44.pdf

88. In one project with Financial Advisors in a UK bank, after cross validation, a combination of biodata metrics and key personality dimensions delivered respectable selection outcomes and business impact. Two years later, the financial regulator changed the rules on compliance and the role of the Financial Advisor changed. The formula broke down.

89. Lyle Ungar on forecasting;
https://intelligence.org/2014/03/26/lyle-ungar/

90. On Amazon and AI in recruitment;
https://becominghuman.ai/amazons-sexist-ai-recruiting-tool-how-did-it-go-so-wrong-e3d14816d98e

91. Amazon Created a Hiring Tool Using A.I. It Immediately Started Discriminating Against Women;
https://slate.com/business/2018/10/amazon-artificial-intelligence-hiring-discrimination-women.html

92. The opportunities and challenges of mitigating bias in AI;
https://www.thetimes.co.uk/static/ai-bias-job-hunting-ibm-recruitment-sexism-discrimination/
https://www.technologyreview.com/s/612876/this-is-how-ai-bias-really-happensand-why-its-so-hard-to-fix/
https://www.cnbc.com/2018/05/30/silicon-valley-is-stumped-even-a-i-cannot-remove-bias-from-hiring.html
https://www.theguardian.com/technology/2019/apr/16/artificial-intelligence-lack-diversity-new-york-university-study

93. The Accuracy of Combining Judgemental and Statistical Forecasts;
https://pubsonline.informs.org/doi/10.1287/mnsc.32.12.1521

94. Can and should employers use handwriting analysis (graphology) in the hiring process?
https://www.linkedin.com/pulse/can-should-employers-use-handwriting-analysis-graphology-ben-riley/
Graphology in selection and assessment;
https://huract.ch/graphology-in-selection-and-assessment/

95. The Validation Crisis in Psychology;
https://replicationindex.com/2019/02/16/the-validation-crisis-in-psychology/

96. Psychology's Replication Crisis Is Running Out of Excuses;
https://www.theatlantic.com/science/archive/2018/11/psychologys-replication-crisis-real/576223

97. Sternberg, R. J., & Williams, W. (1998). Your proved our point better than we did: A reply to our critics. American Psychologist, 53 (5)

98. Fisher, David and Cunningham, Sydnie and Kerr, Alison J. and Allscheid, Steven P., Contextualized Personality Measures in Employee Selection: Extending Frame-of-Reference Research with Job Applicant Samples (March 2017). International Journal of Selection and Assessment, Vol. 25, Issue 1, pp. 18-35, 2017

99. Narrow Reasoning about the Use of Broad Personality Measures for Personnel Selection; Sampo V. Paunonen, Mitchell G. Rothstein and Douglas N. Jackson Journal of Organizational Behavior

100. A new personality trait has been discovered. The need for Drama. I'm quite breathless with this breakthrough finding; http://www.sciencedirect.com/science/article/pii/S01918869150 06327

101. Jingle jangle in personality assessment. Intuitive Talent Management; 10 Guiding Principles For Practitioners; https://talentworldconsulting.com/wp-content/uploads/2023/09/Intuition-In-Talent-Management-Principles.pdf
How similar are personality scales of the same construct? A meta-analytic investigation. Personality and Individual

Differences, 49, 7, 669-676.
https://doi.org/10.1016/j.paid.2010.06.014

102. Grit seems to be largely a combination (repackaging) of the constructs of conscientiousness and emotional stability. Grit correlates around 0.7 or thereabouts. After the hype, a massive back pedal for Grit as a measure in selection. With questions like: "I finish whatever I begin" it is hardly surprising Grit lacks grit as a practical selection tool.
Author Angela Duckworth puts on the brakes. Grit isn't ready for prime time, if prime time means high-stakes tests;
http://www.npr.org/sections/ed/2015/05/13/405891613/a-key-researcher-says-grit-isnt-ready-for-high-stakes-measures

103. Nomothetic Vs Idiographic Approaches In Psychology
https://www.simplypsychology.org/nomothetic-idiographic.htmlNomothetic Approach

104. Everybody lies: how Google search reveals our darkest secrets;
https://www.theguardian.com/technology/2017/jul/09/everybody-lies-how-google-reveals-darkest-secrets-seth-stephens-davidowitz

105. On snoop-ology;
https://www.theguardian.com/science/2008/jun/28/psychology
A Room with a cue: Personality judgments based on offices and bedrooms, Journal of Personality and Social Psychology, 2002

106. Watson's Personality Insights; https://personality-insights-demo.ng.bluemix.net/ But not without reservations: https://medium.com/taraaz/https-medium-com-taraaz-human-rights-implications-of-ibm-watsons-personality-insights-942413e81117

107. When we turn to hiring, employers are missing the forest for the trees. Obsessed with new technologies and driving down costs, they largely ignore the ultimate goal: making the best possible hires. Your Approach to Hiring Is All Wrong; https://hbr.org/2019/05/recruiting
At this point it is tempting to ask: why not simply toss a coin and rely on random selection? After all, it seems to work pretty well in promotion. Head to head evaluation of different systems for promotion in which random selection holds its own. Promotion Systems And Organizational Performance: A Contingency Model; http://citeseerx.ist.psu.edu/viewdoc/download?doi=10.1.1.295.2049&rep=rep1&type=pdf

108. The link to independent research from HireVue's website is unavailable; https://www.prnewswire.com/news-releases/independent-research-reveals-hirevue-drastically-improves-quality-of-hire-recruiter-productivity-and-candidate-experience-252622521.html

109. Personality tests shift towards the kind of design used in biodata measures; Harold, Crystal M. and McFarland, Lynn A.

and Weekley, Jeff A., The Validity of Verifiable and Non-Verifiable Biodata Items: An Examination Across Applicants and Incumbents. International Journal of Selection and Assessment This is also the re-emergence of Cattell's much neglected T data; Santacreu, J., Rubio, V. J., & Hernández, J. M. (2006). The objective assessment of personality: Cattells's T-data revisited and more. Psychology Sciencement Review 23(3)

110. Projective testing: Historical foundations and uses for human resources management; Human Resource Management

111. But no research evidence to back this claim; https://thecambridgecode.com/overview/

112. More Than Meets the Eye: The Evolution of Personality Testing; https://blogs.scientificamerican.com/observations/more-than-meets-the-eye-the-evolution-of-personality-testing/ Visual methodologies in personality test construction; https://d13kjz344z5e1m.cloudfront.net/wp-content/uploads/2014/10/CRWhitepaper_web.pdf

113. On gamification. Game-like personality testing: An emerging mode of personality assessment, Personality and Individual Differences, 2019, https://digest.bps.org.uk/2019/05/15/an-exciting-new-approach-to-personality-testing-involves-psychologists-analysing-your-decisions-in-game-scenarios/ Serious Games for Assessment: Welcome to the Jungle; http://www.jattjournal.com/index.php/atp/article/view/118669

The Truth About Game-based Talent Assessments; https://www.ere.net/the-truth-about-game-based-talent-assessments/

114. Virtual Reality as an Emerging Methodology for Leadership Assessment and Training; https://www.frontiersin.org/articles/10.3389/fpsyg.2018.01658/full

115. Pitfalls of Personality Theory, Colin Cooper. How Not To Discover A Personality Trait; https://www.sciencedirect.com/science/article/abs/pii/S0191886919304830
Cooper's critique is also a challenge to the test publishers whose manuals incorporate more pages on construct validity than genuine predictive validity in selection.

116. More on personality testing and adverse impact; Employment Tests and Employment Discrimination: A Dissenting Psychological Opinion; https://pdfs.semanticscholar.org/2d38/f22fbcf39c30d7a06fdc590d6c801cfc4b2d.pdf
Recent EEOC Actions Show Dangers of Using Personality Tests in Hiring Process; https://www.jdsupra.com/legalnews/recent-eeoc-actions-show-dangers-of-92292/

117. Beware These Marketing Trends in Psychological Assessment; https://www.psychologytoday.com/gb/blog/the-situation-

lab/201910/beware-these-marketing-trends-in-psychological-assessment

118. Rachid Laajaj et al. Challenges to capture the big five personality traits in non-WEIRD populations, Science Advances (2019); https://advances.sciencemag.org/content/5/7/eaaw5226

Printed in Great Britain
by Amazon

37331719R00086